The Bulls

The Bulls

A Season To Remember

Chicago Sun-Times
and
Bonus Books, Inc.

© **1991 by the Chicago Sun-Times, Inc.**

95 94 93 92 91   5 4 3 2 1

Library of Congress Catalog Card Number: 91–73494

International Standard Book Number: 0–929387–40–6

Co-Published by:

Bonus Books, Inc.
160 East Illinois Street
Chicago, Illinois 60611

and

Chicago Sun-Times, Inc.
401 N. Wabash
Chicago, Illinois 60611

Credits

Don Snider, executive sports editor

Staff writers who covered the Bulls: Lacy Banks, Terry Boers, Dave Hoekstra, Mike Mulligan, Ray Sons, Brian Hewitt

Staff photographers who covered the Bulls: Tom Cruze, Robert A. Davis, Brian Jackson, Bob Ringham, Phil Velasquez, Bob Black, Jon Sall

Cover design by Roy Moody. Cover photo by Robert H. Davis. Back cover photo by Jon Sall.

Composition by Point West, Inc., Carol Stream, IL

Printed in the United States of America

Contents

1

The Regular Season

Book it.

The 1990–91 Bulls' championship season had storybook characteristics. A dozen athletes turned pages of personal joys into team glories under the emotional editing of coach Phil Jackson and his assistants.

Every month was a new chapter of growing desire and destiny.

"The experience of being a professional basketball player is a great life," Jackson said on the eve of the deciding Game 5 of the NBA Finals. "There are not many other things that can beat this occupation when you're in your 20s. But there's something about being closed off and not seeing the rest of life—about being enamored with the fact that your cares are taken care of in these arenas.

"So what's important is for my players to get around and see life has other experiences than basketball. That's why I give them books. The important thing about giving books is for companionship. Books are something to be enjoyed. Not all the time do you need to have the television on and be ruminating with friends about past joys and glories on the court."

Here are the Bulls' many joys and glories of the 1990–91 season:

The table-setting story out of training camp was Jackson sitting down with Michael Jordan and asking the NBA's premier showman to temper his show.

"Michael and I sat down and I told him, 'I hope you don't feel pressure to win your fifth

By Dave Hoekstra

ALL EVERYTHING: NBA scoring leader Michael
Jordan won it all—regular season and NBA Finals
MVP and was all-NBA defensive team member.
Photo by Phil Velasquez

PAX MAN: Guard John Paxson had his most consistent season—he was 10th in NBA field goal percentage. *Photo by Robert A. Davis*

scoring title in a row','' Jackson said in mid-October. ''We also discussed the fact there haven't been many NBA championship teams who had the league scoring leader.''

Jackson cited research he had done. Since the 24-second clock was introduced in 1954, only Kareem Abdul-Jabbar, in 1971 with the Milwaukee Bucks, had led the league in scoring the same season his team won an NBA title.

Jordan responded, ''I work day in and day out to make my body stronger so I can continue to play down the stretch. It's going to be hard to tell me not to shoot when I feel I'm open.''

Jordan won his fifth straight scoring title,

but the key statistic was that he scored a smaller percentage of his team's points. The Bulls won the NBA title. And unless he gets injured, Jordan will win a sixth consecutive scoring title.

Book it.

Once the season started, the Bulls didn't. They stumbled to an 0–3 start and the real men were wearing red—faces, that is. The Bulls' third loss in a row came at the Stadium when Boston's Brian Shaw converted a 15-foot Robert Parish prayer with one–tenth of a second left to give the Celtics a 110–108 victory.

The Bulls got their first victory of the season the next night when they beat the Minnesota Timberwolves 96–91 in Minneapolis. "They play basketball like watching paint dry," Jackson said after the game.

So can a team have a big victory this early in the season?

The Bulls answered that question with a resounding *yes* on Nov. 9 when their bench came to the rescue to defeat the Celtics 120–100 before a Friday night sellout at Boston Garden.

B.J. Armstrong had 16 points, Stacey King 14, Dennis Hopson 13 and Cliff Levingston 12 points and a game-high 12 rebounds. Never again during the season would those four players put together such impressive numbers.

"This was the best bench performance I've seen in the three years I've been here," Jackson said. "It always helps when the bench contributes. It boosts the confidence of the whole team."

The Bulls began their annual West Coast, Chicago Stadium Eviction Tour on Nov. 12 in Salt Lake City. Jordan's 18-foot turnaround jumper at the buzzer gave the Bulls a 84–82 victory against the Utah Jazz. The Bulls were over .500 (4–3) for the first time, but it wouldn't last long.

On their next stop, the Bulls lost 103–93 to the Golden State Warriors at the Oakland Coliseum. Before the game, it was pointed out to Jordan that he had a 22.7 scoring average in the six games he has played at the Coliseum—his lowest average in any of the NBA's 26 are-

FLYING BY: Scott Williams fights his way past Denver's Orlando Woolridge for a basket.
Photo by Robert A. Davis

9

(Left) MAKING HIS OWN MAGIC: Scottie Pippen slams over the Orlando Magic's Terry Catledge.
Photo by Bob Ringham

(Below) BULLS' LONG BOMBER: Craig Hodges became the Bulls' three-point specialist, winning the long-shot contest at the All-Star Weekend.
Photo by Tom Cruze

nas. Jordan went out and scored 14 points. Horace Grant had a dream fulfilled, at least for one evening, and led his team in scoring with 18 points.

Reading between the games.

The Bulls moved from the San Francisco Bay Area to Seattle. Word had gotten out that Jackson passed books out to his players for the long trip that would extend through Thanksgiving. About half the books came from Jackson's personal collection.

He gave Will Perdue *Great Santini*. Craig Hodges received *The Way of the Peaceful Warrior*, a novel about a student at Cal-Berkeley who navigates change within himself. Jordan got *Fever*, a collection of essays written by John Edgar Wideman, who authored the abstract profile of Jordan in the November issue of *Esquire* magazine.

Scottie Pippen was surprised to get a copy of Langston Hughes' compilation of prose and short stories, titled, *The Ways of White Folks*. Pippen smiled and said, "I haven't even started to read it. I already know that [the ways of white folks]."

The Bulls went on to beat the SuperSonics before losing 125–112 the next night to the Portland Trail Blazers in what many people thought was a preview of the NBA Finals. The Bulls fell to 5–5 as the Trail Blazers equaled their best start ever at 9–0.

"I was disappointed in our second unit," Jackson said after the game. "Sometimes that happens, and it will happen more on the road. We're not in synch yet." Through the rest of the season Jackson would refer to "synch" at least 125 more times.

The Bulls closed out the road trip Nov. 24 in a ballyhooed meeting with the fast-broken Denver Nuggets at McNichols Arena. Everyone seemed to expect Jordan to score 100 points—except Jordan. He finished with 38 as the Bulls won 151–145. The Bulls came home with a 4–3 record on the West Coast swing—the first time in 16 years they had a winning record on the

November trip. The Bulls were 7–6 overall and had 11 of their next 13 games at home.

You could sense the good fortune that was stirring around the Bulls when they traveled to Cleveland on Dec. 1. The Cavaliers were picked as a Central Division contender, but on the night before the game, Cavaliers All-Star point guard Mark Price tore the anterior cruciate ligament in his left knee when it got caught in courtside advertising signage in Atlanta. Price was lost for the season and so were the Cavs. The Bulls blew out a disoriented Cleveland team 120–85.

New stadium records.

The Bulls maintained a hot hand in their next game when they scorched the Phoenix Suns 155–127 at the Stadium. The Bulls set a Stadium record for most points in a game. The Bulls put up 106 shots and hit on 67 of them, which was also a Stadium record.

The spread-the-wealth offense Jackson suggested in the pre-season was evident in that game. Who would have thought that in a game in which the Bulls scored 155 points that Jordan would finish with only 27? Grant tied his career high with 25 points, plus 12 rebounds. And seven Bulls scored in double figures.

A tidy seven-game winning streak was stopped Dec. 8 when the Trail Blazers beat the Bulls 109–101 at the Stadium. The Bulls trailed 33–30 when Armstrong, Hopson, Perdue and Levingston entered the game with Grant. By the time Jordan returned with fellow first-unit members, the Bulls were down 44–32 midway through the second quarter. The Bulls fell to 12–7, while the Trail Blazers were smoking with an 18–1 record.

The annual Christmas party for underprivileged children was held after practice Dec. 10 at the Deerfield Multiplex. Santa Claus made a surprise appearance and he was confronted by Grant, who admitted, "I asked Santa for about 10 more jump shots per game and a few more wins."

The Bulls had holiday smiles on their faces

SITTING BULL: Dennis Hopson was acquired
before the season to give depth at guard.
Photo by Brian Jackson

the night of Dec. 15. They were playing the
Cavaliers, this time at the Stadium. The Bulls
jumped to a 36–5 first-quarter lead, setting a
club record for holding an opponent to fewest
points in a quarter.

"Wasn't that something?" Jackson asked after the game. "Defensively, I've never seen a
team play a better 10 or 11 minutes of basketball. When you play defense like that, it is an
infectious moment and a psychological high
for the team."

Three nights later, the Bulls would pay their
only visit to the brink in a charmed 1990–91
season. They had been spending weeks aiming
at their first meeting with the Detroit Pistons,
who had eliminated them in the Eastern Conference finals the two previous seasons. Al-
though the Pistons were in the midst of their
worst slump in five years, they beat up the
Bulls 105–84 at the Palace of Auburn Hills.

After the game a disturbed Jackson hinted at
changes.

"I don't know what the problem is," said
Jackson, whose team's record fell to 15–9. "We
sure didn't shoot well (35 percent). Over
Christmas we will have to beat this team. If we
don't, we will have to adjust our team one way
or another."

Turning it around.

The Bulls rebounded to beat their future
NBA Finals opponent, the Los Angeles Lakers,
114–103, and the Indiana Pacers 128–118 in
consecutive weekend games at the Stadium.

Christmas, 1990, was a big deal in the Bulls'
family.

At 5:30 a.m. Christmas Eve, Juanita Jordan
gave birth to 6-pound, 7-ounce Marcus James

BULL RUN: B.J. Armstrong heads up court against the Lakers in their December game. He was the team's top reserve guard, scoring almost 9 points a game.
Photo by Bob Ringham

(Right) ELBOW ROOM: Bulls center Bill Cartwright elbows Golden State's Alton Lister. Cartwright's elbows were a center of controversy during the season. Houston's Hakeem Olajuwan caught one and missed several weeks of action. Cartwright insisted he meant no harm.
Photo by Robert A. Davis

Jordan. Then on Christmas Day, Michael Jordan scored 37 points to lead the Bulls to an important 98–86 victory over the Pistons. The Bulls (18–9) moved a half game behind the Milwaukee Bucks in the Central Division. The Pistons (16–11) were in third place.

The Bulls opened 1991 in the Lone Star State and were jettisoned 114–92 by the Houston Rockets. It would be the Bulls' worst loss of the season. The most memorable thing about the loss was Bill Cartwright's third-quarter TKO of the Rockets' Akeem Olajuwon with an elbow to the head. Olajuwon was never the same. When he returned later in the season, he changed his first name to Hakeem.

On Jan. 9 in Philadelphia, Jordan scored the 15,000th point of his career in a 107–99 victory over the 76ers. In 460 games, Jordan was the second fastest player to reach that milestone. Only Wilt Chamberlain was faster, scoring 15,000 in 358 games. Jordan also had his 500th career blocked shot on Jan. 9. The Bulls' record improved to 23–10.

The Bulls finally ascended into first place in the Central Division on Jan. 13 with a 106–95 victory at Charlotte. The Bulls were 25–10 and for the first time in the season they began talking in title terms.

"I think we are a championship-caliber team," Jordan said after the game against Charlotte. "We came close last year and we can only get better with experience."

Fast forward to Feb. 3 at the Great Western Forum in Los Angeles, where the Bulls would lose for the last time in a long while. The Lakers won their 15th consecutive game in defeating the Bulls 99–86, playing the fourth quarter without Magic Johnson. The Lakers' All-Star guard suffered a concussion and slight amnesia after tripping over teammate Terry Teagle and getting kicked in the head by Horace Grant. Bill Cartwright was innocent. He did not play.

As the Lakers tied the second longest winning streak in club history, the (30–14) Bulls were about to embark on an 11-game winning streak of their own. There were some important turning points during the streak:

■ Before the Bulls' 108–97 victory at Sacramento on Feb. 4, Jackson talked about how assistant coach John Bach spliced together a videotape depicting the multi-dimensional game of Portland Trail Blazers forward Buck Williams. Jackson showed the tape to

Horace Grant, a longtime fan of Williams—a power forward who doesn't worry about scoring but does worry about playing the lane.

■ Just before the Feb. 8 All-Star break, the Bulls beat the Pistons 95–93 at the Palace of Auburn Hills. It was the Bulls' first regular-season triumph in the Palace. The Pistons played without Isiah Thomas, who sat out because of an injured wrist. Still, the Bulls' hearts and minds would consider this the team's most important victory of the season. "We began to have confidence in what we could do," Jackson said in reviewing the season.

(Below) CLIFF HANGER: Cliff Levingston, acquired as a free agent in October, proved to be a valuable reserve forward. *Photo by Brian Jackson*

■ Michael Jordan went home to appear in the NBA All-Star Game at Charlotte, North Carolina. Charles Barkley was named the game's MVP, which was about the only honor Jordan failed to win this season.

■ After the break the Bulls picked up their streak where they left off. On Feb. 20 they beat the Washington Bullets 118–113 at the Stadium. It was their 16th consecutive home victory, which established a franchise record. The Bulls' overall record was 37–14, placing them two games over the Pistons and within 1½ games of the Celtics for Eastern Conference leadership.

■ The Bulls walloped the Sacramento Kings 129–82 on Feb. 22 at the Stadium in a game Kings coach Dick Motta didn't attend because of illness. It was the Bulls' largest margin of victory in the season and the second highest in team history.

■ On the heels of going public with his contract problems, Scottie Pippen had a career night in leading the Bulls to a 129–108 victory over Charlotte on Feb. 23 at the Stadium. Pippen had 43 points on 16-of-17 shooting from the field. In the first quarter alone, Pippen was 8-for-8 from the field with four steals and two assists.

■ The Bulls achieved Eastern Conference leadership with a 129–99 whipping of the Celtics on Feb. 26 at the Stadium. Pippen continued his hot shooting with 33 points, knocking down 14 of 18 shots from the floor. "The Bulls treated this game as if it were the playoffs," said Celtics coach Chris Ford, unknowingly peeking into the future. It was the Bulls' 10th victory in a row and a then-record 19th straight at the Stadium. The Bulls closed out February with a 11–1 record, the best month in team history.

■ The Bulls' 11-game winning streak ended March 2 with a 135–114 loss at Indiana. The streak was one short of the club record, established in 1973. It was the Bulls' sixth consecutive loss in Indianapolis. The team's overall record dropped to 41–15.

The Indiana loss only momentarily stalled the Bulls' momentum.

On March 5 they pounded the Milwaukee Bucks 104–86, and on March 8 they handled the Utah Jazz 99–89, both victories at the Stadium. The victory against the Jazz was the Bulls' 1,000th in club history. On March 10, the Bulls won 122–87 at Atlanta. Jordan and Jackson credited the 11 a.m. starting time (for national television) for the Bulls' savage showing.

"I really like to get out of bed and just go play," Jordan said, who made 10 of 13 shots from the floor. "I don't have to worry and think about the game all day."

The Bulls came home on March 12 and beat the Minnesota Timberwolves 131–99 for the 100th NBA coaching victory in Phil Jackson's career. The Bulls increased their Eastern Conference-leading record to 45–15, having lost just once since the All-Star break.

With a dramatic 102–101 victory March 13 at Milwaukee, the Bulls became the best they could be. Their record improved to 46–15 (.754), which was tops in the NBA at the time. Portland was second at 46–16 (.742). The Bulls won when Frank Brickowski's potential game-winning 22-foot jump shot at the buzzer was ruled a two-point field goal by officials.

"Do I believe in destiny?" Jordan asked after the game. "Yes. Going through it, you think about it. You think about ways of winning and you dream of them making mistakes that you can take advantage of."

John Paxson also gave a hint of how he responds under pressure. He brought the Bulls back with a pair of clutch three-pointers during the last 1:28 of the game.

The Bulls won their 50th game of the season and their 25th consecutive game at the Stadium on March 20, 129–107 over Atlanta. Eight Bulls scored in double figures. Jordan had 22

TEN VS. TEN: B.J. Armstrong eludes Atlanta Hawks' John Battle for a shot. Armstrong had his best game against the Hawks, scoring 19 points in the March 10 game.
Photo by Brian Jackson

points on just 16 shots. He had been averaging 22 shots a game.

Ironically, Bulls players began posting Reggie Miller's quote from Indianapolis, where he had said, "Trade Michael Jordan off that team and who do they have?...Nobody."

So both the Pacers and the Bulls were revved up March 23 at the Stadium. The Bulls beat the Pacers 133–119 in a game in which Pacers Detlef Schrempf and Chuck Person were ejected.

The Bulls led 106–100 with 8:59 left in the game when Person fouled Will Perdue underneath the Bulls' basket. After the whistle, Per-

WILL POWER: Seven-foot Will Perdue goes
against the Lakers' Vlade Divac in their December
meeting.
Photo by Bob Ringham

son plunked the basketball at Perdue's head. That earned Person a second technical and automatic ejection.

The mezzanine kicks.

As Person walked off the court, he kicked the game ball into the west mezzanine seats. A fan threw the ball back. Person retrieved the ball and punted a much better kick into the east mezzanine, forever becoming a part of Stadium lore. Perhaps that's why the Bulls so steeply increased the price of mezzanine seats for the 1991–92 season.

The Bulls' 26-game home winning streak ended in a 100–90 loss March 25 to the Houston Rockets. The Bulls' streak placed them in a tie for second place in the NBA record book with the 1977–78 Portland Trail Blazers and the 1988–89 New York Knicks. The 1985–86 Boston Celtics hold the homecourt streak record of 31 victories.

Heading down the home stretch, the Bulls lost to the Celtics 135–132 in double overtime on March 31 at Boston Garden in one of the most exciting games in franchise history.

The Celtics (52–20) had to beat the Bulls (53–18) to stay in the hunt for Eastern Conference leadership. Reggie Lewis' three-pointer with 19 seconds left in regulation sent the game into overtime.

With the score tied at 118 and 0.4 seconds left in the first overtime, Jordan's desperation shot from in front of the Celtics' bench was ruled no good as time ran out. Larry Bird buried the Bulls in the second overtime, making all four of his field-goal tries. John Paxson had a career-high 28 points, including a 5-for-5 performance from three-point land.

The Bulls rebounded to beat the Orlando Magic 106–102 on April 2 at the Stadium despite Stacey King's walkout from practice the day before the game. King was suspended without pay for the Magic game. King was unhappy about his lack of playing time.

Pippen, meanwhile, still was having prob-

MR. BILL, IF YOU WILL: Bill Cartwright lays it in against the Pacers.
Photo by Brian Jackson

lems with his stalled contract renegotiations. On the same day that King walked, Pippen talked. "If they don't finish my negotiations, then I don't want them to give me a contract and you can quote me," Pippen said. "I want them to trade me to another team after this season. I'm sure I can get my money elsewhere."

(Left) BULL BY THE HORNS: Horace Grant covered the Bulls' forward position well this season. *Photo by Robert A. Davis*

(Below) KING OF THE BULLS: Backup center Stacey King only started six games, but the Bulls won five of them. *Photo by Brian Jackson*

BASKET BOUND: Forward Scottie Pippen drives against Milwaukee.
Photo by Brian Jackson

(Right) COME FLY WITH ME...That was a top-selling video cassette that Michael Jordan also produced. *Photo by Robert A. Davis*

In winning 103–94 against Milwaukee April 15 at the Stadium, the Bulls set a franchise record for most victories in a season—58. The Bulls increased their Eastern Conference lead over the Celtics to 1½ games with three to play.

And the Bulls captured the Eastern Conference in their next game, a 111–101 victory April 17 at Miami. They set another milestone April 19 when they won 115–99 at Charlotte and became the ninth team in NBA history to win 60 games.

The Bulls entered the playoffs as more than a charmed team.

They were a team that had matured together in the rigorous course of the regular season.

"This is a growth period," said Jackson. "These guys grow from being boys to men in the game of basketball. Sometimes it takes three to five years for a guy to make that stretch, until they reach a point where they really know how to take care of themselves and their game. That is what the art of coaching is."

The most artful part of the Bulls' season was ahead of them.

And you had a sense you could book it.

2

The Playoffs

Call it the chronicle of a wreath foretold. On a Thursday night in late April, the Bulls opened the NBA playoffs with a 41-point victory over the visiting New York Knicks.

The game offered perfect foreshadowing of what was to come—to both New York and the rest of the NBA.

The Bulls' swarming defense—which would later befuddle the Philadelphia 76ers, Detroit Pistons and Los Angeles Lakers—reared its beautiful, trapping head in Game 1 against New York, forcing the Knicks into 27 turnovers that translated into 49 points for the Bulls.

Scottie Pippen began his personal playoff mission with 25 points, seven rebounds and four steals to key the 126–85 drumming of the hapless New Yorkers. Michael Jordan was con-tent to watch the game from the sidelines after scoring 28 points in 32 minutes.

"It was really too easy," a wary Phil Jackson said afterward.

Not to worry, oh wise, wide-shouldered one. The Bulls made it all look easy in the Eastern Conference playoffs.

The Knicks bowed 89–79 in Game 2, despite a 42–30 rebounding advantage. Patrick Ewing, who had been stifled in Game 1, shot 7-of-14 in the first half before being tag-teamed by the Bill and Will pivot show into 1-of-8 shooting the rest of the game.

"We don't want to spend any more time in New York than we have to," Scottie Pippen said of the Bulls' first road playoff game.

No wonder. Craig Hodges was charged $47

By Mike Mulligan

for a hamburger and soft drink at the team hotel. Pocketbooks be praised, the Bulls swept through town in a hurry.

A 103–94 victory at Madison Square Garden gave the Bulls the best-of-three series and their first playoff sweep in 10 years. Nine players scored as the Bulls capped the series. In the three games, the Bulls forced 66 turnovers and limited the usually dunk-happy Ewing to 18-of-45 shooting and 11 turnovers.

"We waited for them to break their own back," Pippen said.

Ouch... Next victim.

Philadelphia, here we come.

"Don't nobody want to play us in the playoffs," Philadelphia's Charles Barkley observed after his team swept Milwaukee in its opening playoff series. Certainly Bulls fans were concerned by the matchup—especially because the 76ers had won three of four regular-season meetings, including two at the Stadium. In addition, the team from the city of Brotherly Love was renowned for its open physical hostility.

"Philadelphia is nothing to sneeze at," Phil Jackson warned.

The 76ers resembled the Bulls of old in Game 1 of the series. Charles Barkley, doing his best to fulfill the Michael Jordan role, scored 36 points and grabbed 11 rebounds. Nonetheless, the Bulls led by as many as 26 points before settling for a 105–92 victory.

"It is embarrassing to get beat like that," Barkley said.

In Game 2, the Bulls double- and triple-teamed Barkley. That helped guard Hersey Hawkins to shake free for 30 points. But because all five starters scored in double figures, the Bulls built a 62–53 halftime lead and cruised to a 112–100 victory.

WHO'S BAD NOW? Michael Jordan battles for a rebound against the Pistons' Bill Laimbeer (left) and Joe Dumars. The Bulls bounced the NBA's "Bad Boys" in four games.
Photo by Robert A. Davis

The post-season was flowing along just swimmingly until Friday, May 10. In their first playoff game decided by fewer than 10 points, the Bulls lost 99–97 as Hawkins, a native Chicagoan, made a three-pointer with 10.3 seconds left.

"The game was there for us to win," said Jordan, who scored 46 points but missed two free

throws in the final 84 seconds before making two to give the Bulls a 97–95 lead with 15 seconds left. ''We had every opportunity.''

Pippen missed an ill-advised, off-balance 17-footer in the waning seconds before Armon Gilliam made a free throw for the final score.

On that same day the Bulls also lost their celebrated draft pick, Yugloslav star Toni Kukoc, who opted to sign with Benetton of the Italian league for a reported $25 million over six years. The Bulls and their reported six-year, $16 million offer lost out, but there's hope: Kukoc has an escape clause after each year of the Italian contract.

None of the Bulls seemed too concerned—about the loss or about Kukoc.

WILL POWER: Backup center Will Perdue distinguished himself in the playoff series against the Sixers.
Photo by Tom Cruze

The Bulls bounced back, buoyed by balance in Game 4. Three starters scored at least 20 points—Jordan 25, Horace Grant 22 and Pippen 20—in a 101–85 romp.

Grant also had 11 rebounds, including seven offensive.

"What are our chances for a comeback?" Barkley asked. "I'm not going to lie to you. It's going to be a long, hard, row for us to hoe."

The Bulls returned to the Stadium for Game 5 with the intention of finishing off the 76ers in order to get some extra rest before taking on the Pistons-Celtics winner in the Eastern Conference final. Jordan was bothered by tendinitis in his left knee, Paxson had a sore wrist and Cartwright's knees were aching.

"A sweep would have been nice," Jordan lamented.

They got the next best thing, beating the 76ers 100–95 for a 4–1 series victory. Pippen opened the show by making his first nine field-goal attempts en route to scoring 24 of his 28 points in the first half. Jordan brought down the curtain by scoring 12 of his 38 points in the last six minutes. Sore knee and all, Jordan grabbed a playoff career-high 19 rebounds to lead the Bulls to a 52–29 rebounding advantage.

"In the end it was just a good team effort," Jordan said.

Said 76ers coach Jim Lynam: "Your fear is always that Michael will take over the game like he did."

Detroit: how sweet it was.

The Bulls next playoff obstacle proved to be the one they had been unable to negotiate in years past—the dreaded, hated, irreverent and ultimately unsportsmanlike Detroit Pistons.

The two-time defending NBA champions strutted into Chicago with their usual mixture of bravado, confidence, cockiness and arrogance. For the Bulls, the playoffs had finally, truly arrived. This was the series they had been waiting for, and this was the team they wanted to beat more than any other.

"All year long they've been saying they want to play us," Detroit's Isiah Thomas said. "Well, here we are."

Thomas and his cohorts talked like that right to the bitter end. It seemed the more the Bulls dismantled the Pistons' war machine, the less respect the Motowners showed.

Jordan, for one, had clearly had enough of the trash-talking Pistons. He got a bit mouthy

KEEP AWAY: Sixers' Charles Barkley tries to keep
the ball away from Scottie Pippen. But
Philadelphia couldn't keep the Bulls from
advancing in the playoffs.
Photo by Robert A. Davis

himself while leading the Bulls to a 94–83 victory in Game 1.

"He kept telling me I couldn't stop him," Pistons defensive specialist Dennis Rodman said. "I said: 'You're right, I can't stop you. If I was you, could you stop me?'

"Then his teammates started saying (to Jordan): 'Tell him who you are.' I said, 'I think I know who he is.'

"He doesn't usually talk...I guess he was trying to prove he can go out there and be physical and be a tough guy."

The Bulls' bench had a point to prove as well. After being bad-mouthed all year, it was the spark off the bench that ignited the Game 1 victory. Reserves B.J. Armstrong, Craig Hodges, Will Perdue and Cliff Levingston joined starter Horace Grant in a 13–7 fourth-quarter run that extended a three-point lead while Jordan and Pippen were resting.

"You have to give my supporting cast a lot of credit because I did not have a particularly good game," said Jordan, who finished with 22 points.

Jordan proved in Game 2 you can't keep a good Air-man grounded. He soared for 35 points, including 15 in the fourth quarter. The pugnacious Pistons picked up three flagrant fouls, with Joe Dumars, John Salley and Thomas called for one each. Detroit was called for 35 fouls to 20 for the Bulls. Those calls led Salley to observe, "Rumors and deductions are already embedded in some people's minds."

Said Rodman: "The whole Bad Boy thing is a myth."

It seemed just that—Detroit's starting front line was outscored 41–10.

"We're preparing ourselves for a dogfight," Jordan said of the series' shift to Detroit.

The Bulls rushed to an early lead in Game 3 as they had done in the previous two victories in Chicago. But it was fourth-quarter poise that sealed the 113–107 victory. Jordan shot 5-of-5 from the field in scoring 14 points in the final quarter. He also forced Joe Dumars into a terrible shot off a two-on-one breakaway with 1:45

left that could have closed the lead to three points.

Pippen further shook off the ghost of play-offs past with a 26-point, 10-rebound performance. B.J. Armstrong made a crucial three-pointer late in the game that stemmed a Pistons' run. Most of all, the Bulls were unruffled by the pushing, shoving, cheap-shot tactics the Pistons employed.

"We've matured," Pippen said. "While they're out there throwing the cheap shots and elbows, we try to play basketball."

It was on a Memorial Day in late May that the Pistons saw their three-peat hopes end in four-closure. The Bulls swarmed to a 115–94 victory, ending the Pistons' era of thuggery.

Only John Salley had the grace to congratulate Jordan on the victory. Isiah Thomas, Bill Laimbeer and Co. didn't stick around for the final seconds, taking an early exit to their locker room as only a posturing Piston can.

But the sheepish grins at the crowds' chants of Go L.A.!, Go L.A.! couldn't spoil the Bulls' moment.

"We beat a rival that has humiliated us in the past, mocked us and beat us physically," Jackson said.

Jordan, who treated the Detroit series as a moral imperative, even calling the Pistons bad for basketball, was especially pleased with the way the Bulls again ignored the Pistons' physical style, which resulted in another flagrant foul and four technicals.

"It was typical," Jordan said.

Pippen was victimized by the most blatant foul of the night when Rodman pushed him out of bounds on a drive to the basket. But Pippen had an answer for that: He scored 23 points, second to Jordan's 29, and had a team-high 10 assists.

"They were definitely taking cheap shots,

(Right) PISTONS NO PROBLEM: Michael Jordan goes against Detroit Pistons' Bill Laimbeer in the playoffs, swept by the Bulls 4-0.
Photo by Bob Black

but that's the Pistons tradition,'' Pippen said. ''We've learned to shake it off and keep playing.''

Said Jordan: ''We were successful because we ignored their style of basketball. This was the hardest route for us to go through—the defending NBA champions. We didn't want it any other way.''

3

The NBA Finals

It was billed as the dream NBA Finals, a matchup that caused almost as much excitement along Madison Street in Chicago as it did on Madison Avenue in New York, where overjoyed television and advertising executives could have danced all night.

Michael vs. Magic, MJ vs. MJ, Legend vs. Legend, the game's most charismatic player vs. the game's most noted ring bearer, a man who had helped lead the "Showtime" Los Angeles Lakers to five world championships.

Last names were strictly optional.

The hypewriters were working overtime in the brief period before the Lakers, who had upset the Portland Trail Blazers in six games in the Western Conference finals, arrived in Chicago to meet the Bulls at the Stadium in Game 1.

"All I know is that my team is playing against the Lakers," Jordan said on the eve of the opener. "I'm not going to take it out of context and try and make it a one-on-one situation or make it anything special."

Not special? Did he say this wasn't special?

That's like saying the Mona Lisa is just a painting, the Golden Gate is just another bridge or the Grand Canyon is just another hole in the ground.

The consensus among the experts in Chicago was that the Bulls, who were making their first appearance in the NBA Finals, would snap, crackle and pop the Lakers in quick fashion, that there was just no stopping this silver anniversary bullet.

Writers from around the country, meanwhile, generally thought the Lakers' big-game

By Terry Boers

experience and Johnson's savvy would be the deciding factor in a series many believed would go the distance.

And unlike so many Super Bowls and World Series of recent vintage, the first game more than lived up to the billing.

While many of the Bulls later would confess to a bad case of addled nerves, they were right in the game until the bitter end, clinging to a 91–89 lead with just less than 24 seconds left to play.

That's when Johnson, who had been shadowed by Jordan throughout the day, sensed a double team coming and whipped the ball to Sam Perkins, who was standing to the right of the key, his toes nearly touching the three-point line.

Perkins, Jordan's teammate on the 1982 national championship team at North Carolina, boldly launched a three-pointer that was per-

(Right) TIP OFF: Bill Cartwright and the Lakers' Vlade Divac get the Finals started.
Photo by Brian Jackson

(Above) SIGN OF THE TIMES: Nine-year-old Seth Cooper roots on his heroes.
Photo by Robert A. Davis

(Below) WARMING UP: Will Perdue hits the court for the pregame shootaround.
Photo by Robert A. Davis

GOT A STEP ON HIM: Michael Jordan drives past
an off-balance Magic Johnson.
Photo by Robert A. Davis

fect, giving Los Angeles a 92–91 lead with 14 seconds left.

"The biggest shot of my career," Perkins called it.

The Bulls still had a chance to regain the lead, but Jordan's jumper from seventeen feet rattled in and out. The Lakers' Byron Scott rebounded the miss and quickly was fouled. He made one of two free throws. Scottie Pippen's desperate halfcourt shot left some hope, but the ball bounced off the rim at the buzzer. Stunning final: Lakers 93, Bulls 91.

"I didn't drive inside because they expected me to drive," Jordan said of his last shot. "Besides, when I drove, I didn't get the foul. Plus, I had a wide-open shot. It felt good. But they all feel good."

What didn't feel good was that the Bulls, who lost for just the second time in 13 playoff games, suddenly had lost the home-court advantage they had worked all season to get. Moreover, they again were being criticized in some quarters as a one-man team, owing in no small part to the fact that Jordan (36 points) and Pippen (19 points) were the only Bulls to finish in double figures. The other starters scored six points apiece, not the kind of six-shooters the Bulls would need.

Game 2 was critical.

With what amounted to a three-day cooling off between games, the Bulls had plenty of time to ponder their situation, to digest the notion that if they didn't win Game 2, they virtually were finished. They also wanted to avoid making a little negative history, for no team had lost the first two games of an NBA Finals series at home.

"The season is right now," Jordan said the day before Game 2. "We know we've got to win. Everything has been leading up to now. We've had important games, like last year in Detroit (in Game 7 of the Eastern Conference finals). But nothing compares to this."

"This will be the biggest game of our careers," John Paxson said. "This is huge."

How the Bulls would respond to what basically was the first bit of adversity they had faced in a charmed season didn't seem to be of much concern to coach Phil Jackson.

"I think this team responds well to challenges and adversity," Jackson said. "They measure up well."

As things turned out, that was just about the size of it.

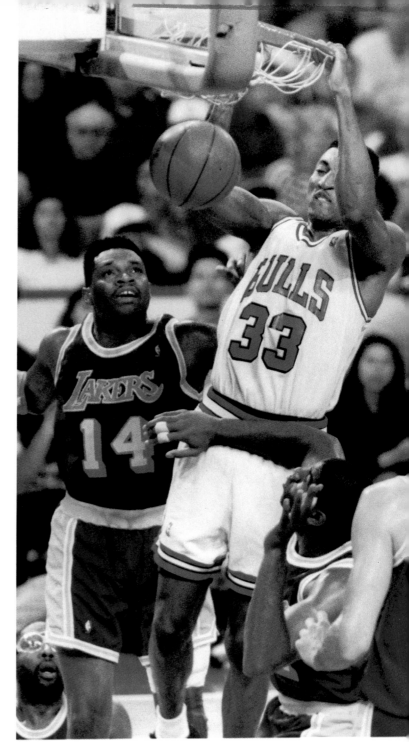

JAM IT: Scottie Pippen hangs on the rim after dunking amid some helpless Lakers.
Photo by Robert A. Davis

Putting together the best shooting night any team ever has had in the NBA Finals, the Bulls raced to a 107–86 victory that wasn't as close as the score indicated.

The Bulls shot .617 to the Lakers' .411, pulling away during a torrid third quarter in which

they made 17 of 20 shots (.850) from the floor. That was enough to turn their 48–43 halftime lead into an 86–69 avalanche. Later, the lead would grow to 97–71.

Jordan, who shot 15-for-18, had 33 points.

(Left) VICTORY: The Lakers exult over their victory in Game 1 after Michael Jordan's shot rolled around the rim and bounced out as time was running out. *Photo by Robert A. Davis*

(Below) THE MATCHUP: Michael Jordan guards Magic Johnson in the first of many battles. *Photo by Brian Jackson*

Horace Grant and Pippen each scored 20 points, Paxson had 16 on 8-for-8 shooting, and Bill Cartwright 12.

"We reached a level of dominance where you feel confident and the team really gets going," Jackson said. "I could tell in the locker room before the game that they had their feet on the ground, that they were ready to play."

But how would things change for the Bulls once they got their feet in the Forum, where they had won only one game in the previous six years? Where they had a 13-game playoff losing streak?

THE POST MAN: Bill Cartwright backs in against Lakers center Vlade Divac.
Photo by Phil Velasquez

Game 3, the series' most pivotal, provided all the answers.

While it was far from being an artistic delight, it was easily the best game of the series. The Lakers, who had been playing with a remarkably close-to-the-vest style, and the Bulls parried and thrust through the entire first half, which ended with the Bulls on top 48–47.

Most of the third quarter belonged to the Lakers, who hit their best offensive stride in building a 69–56 lead.

But as Jordan later would point out, the Lakers ''are known for letting other teams back in the game.''

The Bulls sliced the lead to just six points at the end of the period, then overtook the Lakers early in the fourth quarter, due mainly to their 46–29 rebounding advantage for the game. Those 29 rebounds were the lowest total ever recorded by a team in the Finals. The Lakers had the old mark of 31 against the Detroit Pistons in 1988.

Despite the onslaught, the Lakers held firm, taking a 92–90 lead in the final 10 seconds when center Vlade Divac came rumbling down the lane. Never appearing to be in full control of the ball or himself, Divac still managed to make a layup and draw the sixth foul on Pippen, who left with 19 points and 13 rebounds.

Divac's free throw made it 92–90, with the clock showing 10.9 seconds.

What happened next is a scene that has been repeated countless times during Jordan's career. Getting the ball and heading to the other end of the floor at roughly the speed of light, Jordan, who had suffered through a difficult shooting night, shook free from Scott and pulled up for a 12-footer from the right.

Divac jumped out at him, but it was too little, too late. Jordan's hoop sent the game into overtime tied at 92.

HERE'S JACK: Laker mascot Jack Nicholson screams for justice.
Photo by Robert A. Davis

STAR WARS: Longtime Lakers fan Dyan Cannon can't believe what the Bulls are doing to her team.
Photo by Robert A. Davis

With the Lakers suddenly looking their age, the extra period belonged to the Bulls and Jordan, who had a pair of twisting layups and a pair of free throws as Chicago broke it open, winning 104–96.

"It came down to Michael hitting a tough shot," Lakers coach Mike Dunleavy said. "He hit the shot with the defender all over him. You can't ask for more than that. I wasn't displeased with the shot he got. I was displeased that he made it."

The toe that made headlines.

The one lingering question had to do with the health of Jordan, who jammed the big toe

SKY WALKER: Scottie Pippen flies toward the basket, preparing to dunk over the Lakers' Magic Johnson in Game 5 of the NBA Finals.
Photo by Brian Jackson

on his right foot when he landed awkwardly after making the big basket.

Dr. John Hefferon, the Bulls' team physician, indicated the next day that Jordan, who skipped practice, definitely would play in Game 4, but he wasn't sure how effective Jordan would be.

"We'll see how the toe responds to treatment," Hefferon said.

But on game day, the Lakers were a toe-tal disaster.

Never really in Game 4 after the first quarter,

the Lakers went meekly and mildly, losing 97–82 and falling behind 3–1 in games.

"We're in a ditch," a disgusted Dunleavy said later. "Not a hole. A ditch."

Jordan, meanwhile, made himself whole again in an interesting way.

He started the game wearing a shoe on his right foot that had a two-inch slit cut in the top to relieve pressure on the toe. That was Hefferon's handiwork.

But feeling as if he wasn't getting proper support, Jordan changed back to his regular shoe during the first timeout.

Jordan, who would finish with 28 points and 13 assists, never appeared to be in any distress again. The only time he showed any hint of

WHAT?: Scottie Pippen has to hold back Michael Jordan, who is angry about being whistled for a foul.
Photo by Bob Ringham

pain was when he went up for one of his trademark one-handed jams, this time over the 6–10 Perkins.

"Once I started moving and warming up, the toe didn't hurt as much," Jordan said. "But wearing the cut shoe, my foot felt like it was going to come out of the shoe whenever I pushed off on it."

As bleak as it looked for the Lakers, the situation was made worse when starters James Worthy and Scott were injured.

Worthy, who never had recovered fully from the sprained ankle he suffered in Game 5 of the Western Conference finals, pulled up lame in the third quarter and left the game. In the same period, Scott slipped on a wet spot, fell to the floor and bruised his right shoulder. He, too, missed the fourth quarter.

"This is like a nightmare," a dejected Johnson said. "I never dreamed that this would happen. I never even thought about it—us being dominated like this."

But dominated they were.

And Johnson wasn't doing much better as the four-game returns in the Michael vs. Magic Sideshow came rolling in. Johnson not only was being outscored, as everyone expected he would be, but Jordan also had more assists and was shooting 55 percent from the field to Johnson's 43.

While the Lakers put up a brave front in the days before Game 5, their words seemed to get more hollow as the day approached.

Johnson, whose optimism is generally boundless, even spoke of retiring, claiming he would take a few weeks after the season to determine if he wanted to return.

While he later would leave no doubt he would be back, the Bulls were making sure no one would question which was the better team.

Because Dunleavy found some fresh and willing legs in rookies Elden Campbell and Tony Smith—Worthy and Scott didn't play—Game 5 was tied at 93 with about four minutes left. But then Paxson took over.

SLAM IT: Michael Jordan blows past Magic Johnson and dunks for two points in Game 3 of the NBA Finals.
Photo by Brian Jackson

Scolded a bit by Jordan for missing his shots in Game 1, Paxson went on a shooting tear and scored 10 of the Bulls' next 12 points.

By the time the last rebound came down in the hands of Pippen, who had a game-high 32 points, 13 rebounds, 7 assists and 5 steals, the

celebration of the Bulls' 108–101 championship-clinching victory already had begun.

They danced in the streets of Chicago, and the nation watched as Jordan, who was named the playoff MVP by a unanimous vote, broke down in tears in the locker room.

Flanked by his father, James, and his wife, Juanita, Jordan sobbed uncontrollably as he kissed the gold Larry O'Brien Trophy, emblematic of the NBA championship.

"I've never been this emotional publicly," Jordan said. "But I couldn't help it. I don't know if I'll ever have this same feeling. What you see are the emotions of hard work."

What you also saw was the notion the Bulls are nothing more than a one-man team laid to rest, perhaps permanently.

Just look at the numbers.

The Bulls set all kinds of team records for a five-game Finals, including field-goal percentage (.527), free-throw percentage (.826), most

(Left) JOHNNY ON THE SPOT: John Paxson, guarded by the Lakers' A.C. Green and Magic Johnson, turned in a tremendous championship series with his deadly outside shooting. *Photo by Brian Jackson*

(Below) VINTAGE YEAR: Scottie Pippen pours champagne on Scott Williams. *Photo by Brian Jackson*

BULLS OWN TROPHY: Bulls owner Jerry Reinsdorf (in tie) holds up the NBA championship trophy amid the champagne celebration in the locker room.
Photo by Brian Jackson

assists (139), most steals (49) and fewest turnovers (66).

Contrast that to the Lakers' five-game Finals records, which came for fewest points (458), fewest field goals attempted (374), fewest rebounds (178) and fewest defensive rebounds (119).

''We started from scratch, on the bottom,'' Jordan said. ''It took seven years, but we won. This should get rid of the stigma of the one-man team.''

Two days after the victory, a crowd estimated at anywhere from 300,000 to a million jammed Grant Park to salute their conquering heroes at a noon rally, hosted by Johnny Kerr.

Wearing every type of Bulls paraphernalia imaginable, the fans chanted, sang, clapped and cheered. Oh, how they cheered.

The Bulls shared the podium with other dignitaries, including Governor James Edgar and Mayor Richard Daley.

But Jordan and the Bulls, 15–2 in the playoffs and 76–23 overall, were the kings.

At long last.

BILL & WILL SHOW
Will Perdue gives fellow center
Bill Cartwright a champagne shower

Photo by Brian Jackson

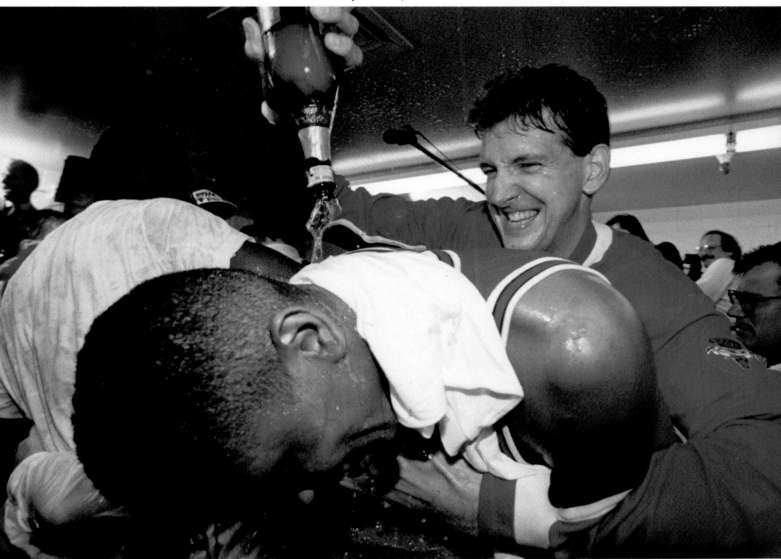

TEARS OF JOY
Michael Jordan breaks down in tears and hugs the championship trophy in the locker room after the Bulls win the championship

Photo by Brian Jackson

4

The Players and Coaches

Michael Jordan was as essential to the Bulls' first NBA championship as beef is to beef stew.

There's more to the stew than the meat, but securing the beef first gives the cook a headstart.

Similarly, when they won the championship, the Bulls proved they were more than a one-man team, more than 100 percent beef. But what a headstart they got when former general manager Rod Thorn selected Jordan third in the first round of the 1984 draft.

"As talent goes, that was an extremely good draft," Thorn said. "It ranks as one of the best ever. Houston had the No. 1 pick and they selected (seven-foot center) Hakeem Olajuwon. If Olajuwon and Jordan had been available when we picked, we would have picked Olajuwon.

"At that time, the prevailing thinking was that 6-foot-6 guys are limited in how good they can be. If you are building a team, you always start by selecting the best center available. Of course, Michael has changed all that."

The Portland Trail Blazers used the No. 2 pick to draft 7-foot Kentucky center Sam Bowie. Had Bowie been available, the Bulls would not have picked him, Thorn said.

If neither Olajuwon nor Jordan had been available, the Bulls probably would have taken Jordan's North Carolina teammate, 6-9 Sam Perkins, who would go No. 4 to Dallas. Or Auburn's 6-6 muscleman Charles Barkley, who would go fifth to Philadelphia. Or Providence's Otis Thorpe, who went ninth to the Kansas City Kings.

Other good players picked later were Kevin

By Lacy J. Banks

(Above) SUN OF A GUN: Michael Jordan does his thing, soaring over the Suns for a slam. *Photo by Brian Jackson*

(Right) C'MON BULLS: Coach Phil Jackson yells from the sidelines. *Photo by Bob Ringham*

Willis (11), Jay Humphries (13), John Stockton (16) and Tony Campbell (20).

But Jordan was available at No. 3.

Jordan, the prodigy who electrified the basketball world as a freshman when he made the

game-winning jumper that enabled the Tar Heels to beat Patrick Ewing and the Georgetown Hoyas for the NCAA championship.

Later, Jordan would become NCAA player of the year and lead the U.S. Olympic team to the gold medal in 1984 in Los Angeles.

"He's the best player in the game," said Indiana's Bobby Knight, who coached that Olympic team.

"Did I know (Jordan) would turn out to be as good as he is?" Thorn said. "No. My feeling was that he was an extraordinary athlete who, at worst, would be a very good NBA player and, at best, would be an All-Star player.

"Of course, Jordan far exceeded my expectations. He has developed into one of the best players I've ever seen. I'm happy I had some small part in bringing him into the league."

Jordan had an excellent rookie year. He led the team in four categories—scoring (averaging 28.2 points a game), rebounds (6.5), assists (5.9) and steals (2.39). He was named Rookie of the Year and the Bulls won 11 more games than the previous year, finishing 38–44.

Not a bad squad.

"From the standpoint of physical talent, that team had more talent than any other I've played with," Jordan said.

They had shooters in Quintin Dailey, Orlando Woolridge and Wes Matthews. Rebounders in Sidney Green, Steve Johnson and David Greenwood. A shot blocker in Jawann Oldham. A penetrator and passer in Ennis Whatley. A good-shooting big man in 6–11 Dave Corzine.

But while the team was long on talent, it was short on the chemistry necessary to win a championship.

In early 1985, the Bulls changed ownership. Jerry Reinsdorf and some new partners purchased the team. Reinsdorf released Thorn and brought in Jerry Krause to run the basketball operation. Krause looked at the team and saw only three or four players, including Jordan, worth keeping.

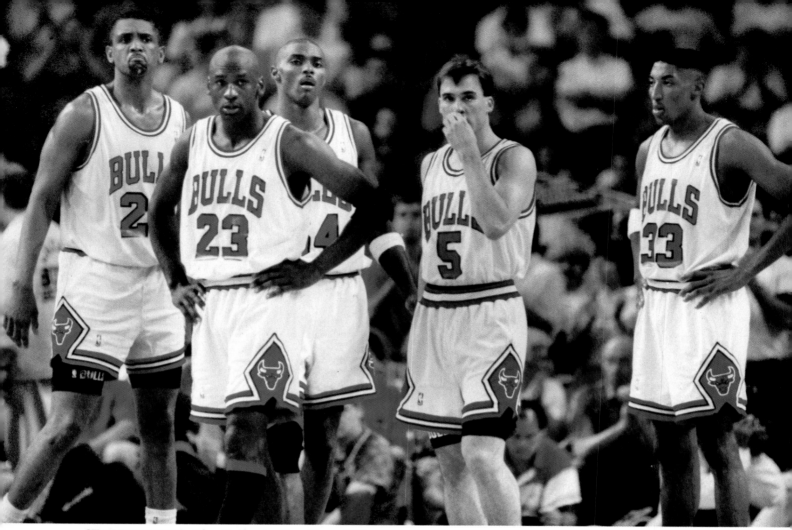

STARTING FIVE: The Bulls starting five—Bill
Cartwright, Michael Jordan, Horace Grant, John
Paxson and Scottie Pippen—remained consistent
throughout the season.
Photo by Phil Velasquez

"I looked at that team and I saw bad chemistry," Krause said. "I saw players who were all
skilled athletes. But they were good players
who could not play good together. I didn't
think there was any pride in the organization.
There was no pride in the uniform. The team
had a lot of characters but very little character.
Plus, we were capped financially.

"We needed to do a complete about-face. We
brought in a whole new staff of coaches and
changed the way we did everything. I brought
in Al Vermeil and Eric Helland as the first
strength and conditioning consultants the
team ever had. We changed training camps. We
moved to a more modern, better equipped fa-
cility."

Krause hired a new coaching staff, headed
by Stan Albeck. But the only survivor from that
staff is assistant Tex Winter, the offensive specialist whom Krause has admired for years.

Krause made 16 deals his first full year. And
the only survivor of those deals is veteran point
guard John Paxson.

"Paxson had the qualities Mr. Reinsdorf and
I were looking for in building the team,"
Krause said. "And he was the ideal complement for Michael. He was a hard worker, an excellent shooter and ballhandler and very
unselfish."

The latter quality was extremely important
for the person who would play opposite the
game's greatest player.

"It's easy for a lot of players to be intimidated by Michael because he is so talented," Paxson said. "I never had that problem. I always saw it as an advantage to be paired with Michael. He makes my game so much easier because of the things he does and the defensive pressure he draws."

"Paxson understands me better than anybody else on the team," Jordan said, "because we've played together longer. He knows when and how I like the ball. I know that he can hit the open shot when I penetrate and draw double-teams."

Enter Coach Jackson.

After two more coaching changes, including the controversial release of popular Doug Collins, Krause entered this season with second-year head coach Phil Jackson, defensive specialist Johnny Bach, former NBA guard Jimmy Cleamons and Winter.

After 20 more player transactions by Krause, the Bulls entered this season with Jordan, Paxson, starting center Bill Cartwright, starting forwards Scottie Pippen and Horace Grant.

The bench comprised centers Will Perdue and Scott Williams, guards B.J. Armstrong, Craig Hodges and Dennis Hopson and forwards Stacey King and Cliff Levingston.

The drafting of 6–7 small forward Pippen (No. 5) and 6–10 power forward Grant (10) in 1987 turned out to be the best acquisitions since Jordan.

Pippen and Grant grew together in the NBA and the Bulls said they felt they would be ready to win the championship when these two players matured around Jordan.

There reportedly was a time when part of management thought that Pippen and Grant were too close and playful off court, that neither would reach his full potential until one was traded.

"Whoever felt that way in management ought to be removed," Grant said. "I admit we were immature when we first came into the

DOUBLE TROUBLE: Scottie Pippen drives against Philadelphia. Pippen had 20 "double-doubles" in which he scored and rebounded in double figures.
Photo by Robert A. Davis

league. We both were country boys moving into the bright lights and fast lanes of city life. We were like kids in a candy store, all excited at what we saw and wanted to sample everything."

But since Pippen underwent surgery to repair a back injury that hampered him his first two years, he has been playing his best ball. He was named an All-Star last year, missed it this season, but used the snub as incentive to play his best in the playoffs.

"I didn't make the All-Star team this year," Pippen said. "But I believe I had an All-Star season."

And the 1990–91 Bulls believed all along they had chemistry.

During the team's annual pre-season luncheon, Jordan looked down the table and said, "I can confidently say that there is not one player on this team that I can't play well with," Jordan said. "This team has the best chemistry of any I've ever played with."

No bad apples.

"There's not a bad apple in the bunch," Krause said. "Everybody on the team, the coaches and the players, carry his own weight. And this team never quits. The coaching staff also is the best in the business. They spend long hours together reviewing films, scouting games, studying opponents and no other coaching staff is better prepared when they take the floor.

"A lot of our games are won in the weight rooms with Al Vermeil and in the coaches' office, where they put together the game plans long before the game is played. I'm extremely proud of our whole staff. I'm talking about unsung heroes like my assistant, Karen Stack; my scouts, Jim Stack and Clarence Gaines; and our European assistant coach and scout, Herb Brown, who is doing a fine job scouting the European market for us."

Krause's selection of the current Bulls was not mere happenstance. After several disappointing acquisitions, Krause became more meticulous about his investigation of the skills, personal backgrounds and personalities of the players. He even has used private detectives to help obtain this information.

In changing from Collins to Jackson, Reinsdorf and Krause said Jackson had the less frenetic, more laid-back personality that would be conducive to the players' reaching their potential.

"Collins did a good job getting us to the point where we could challenge for the title," Reinsdorf said. "Collins took us from point 'A' to point 'B.' But Jackson has the necessary qualities to take us to point 'C.'"

After the Bulls won the championship, rolling through the playoffs winning 15 and losing only 2, Reinsdorf declared Jackson's job a mission accomplished.

"We have now moved to point 'C,'" Reinsdorf said. "That 'C' stands for championship."

It wasn't just that Jackson had a pleasing personality that made it easier for players to play under him. Jackson also incorporated the trapping defense that had as much to do with the Bulls' playoff success as anything else.

Except maybe that kid from North Carolina.

A Glimpse at the 1990-91 Bulls.

1. Michael Jordan, 6-6, off guard: Drafted No. 3 in 1984, Jordan won his fifth consecutive scoring title and won the regular-season MVP award and the NBA Finals MVP award.
2. John Paxson, 6-2, point guard: Signed in 1985 as restricted free agent.
3. Scottie Pippen, 6-7, small forward: Drafted No. 5 in 1987.
4. Horace Grant, 6-10, power forward: Drafted No. 10 in 1987.
5. Bill Cartwright, 7-1, center: Acquired in 1988 from New York with the 11th pick in the '88 draft for power forward Charles Oakley and the No. 16 pick in the first round.
6. Will Perdue, 7-0 center: Drafted No. 11 in 1988. Progressing on both ends of the court, slowly but surely.
7. Craig Hodges, 6-2, shooting guard: Acquired from Phoenix Suns for Ed Nealy, Dec. 14, 1988.
8. Cliff Levingston, 6-8, forward: Signed as unrestricted free agent in summer of 1990. Played best during playoffs.
9. B.J. Armstrong, 6-2, point guard: Gained nine pounds in summerlong conditioning program under strength coach Al Vermeil and was most consistent contributor off the bench during the regular season.
10. Stacey King, 6-11 center: Regressed from rookie season. Boycotted a practice to pro-

test a decrease in playing time. Has asked to be traded.

11. Scott Williams, 6–10 rookie backup center: Started season slowly, but worked enough to be included in regular rotation.

12. Dennis Hopson, 6–5, guard: Had poor season, failing to provide scoring to complement Jordan as management had hoped.

Coaches.

In head coach Phil Jackson and assistants Tex Winter, Johnny Bach and Jim Cleamons, the Bulls' staff has more than 100 years of playing and coaching experience.

KEEPING AN EYE ON BULLS: Phil Jackson takes command of the floor action in his second season as head coach.
Photo by Bob Ringham

5

Epilogue

Along the trail to a basketball championship, memories take root in the mind, to be picked like flowers at your leisure:

- Michael Jordan's most impossible shots. The change of hands and intent from dunk to layup in mid-flight in Game 2 against the Lakers. The solo charge the length of the floor to tie Game 3 and send it into overtime. Jordan spoiling a two-on-one break by the Detroit Pistons that could have turned that series around.

- Magic Johnson lighting the interview room with his smile while acknowledging the Bulls were "unstoppable."

- The Reverend Jesse Jackson hailing this writer in a Los Angeles restaurant to deliver a sermon on Scottie Pippen. He pronounced Pippen the second coming of "Dr. J."

- Jerry Krause, always wearing the same suit, standing in the same spot on the floor under the stands in the Palace of Auburn Hills, Mich., before both road games with Detroit. Superstition demanded he couldn't change, or he might break the magic spell in which his fondest dream was being realized.

It took God only six days to create heaven and earth, while it took seven years to create the champion Bulls.

By Ray Sons

From that, we must assume the builders of Chicago's pro basketball franchise were less than God-like and subject to as many dumb mistakes as the rest of us humans.

The dawn of creation was the day in 1984 when Rod Thorn, then general manager, drafted Jordan, who would turn out to be as much of a deity as anybody in sports.

But it took those seven years to surround Jordan with a chorus of angels in sneakers who could ascend to basketball heaven.

It might never have happened if Jerry Reinsdorf and his investors hadn't bought control of the team in March of 1985.

Reinsdorf moves in mysterious (even weird) ways with his baseball White Sox and the Bulls. Whatever his flaws, he has one great strength: He's the boss.

The basketball franchise had floundered for years under a committee of owners who had too many other interests to devote much time to the Bulls and would not delegate significant authority.

Thorn, now NBA director of operations, couldn't make a major decision as Bulls general manager without consulting an executive committee that often was scattered from the Caribbean to the Dead Sea.

Krause has no such problem. Reinsdorf speaks to him with a single voice of authority. "And Krause doesn't always have to call Reinsdorf," says Johnny Kerr, the Bulls broadcaster and former coach.

Nothing Reinsdorf has done shocked us more than his naming of Krause as vice president/basketball operations, replacing Thorn.

Krause had been involved in scouting and groundwork for deals for four baseball franchises and as many NBA teams. To hear him tell it, he had tipped the Almighty that David had a good arm with a slingshot. But he had never held a job of this magnitude.

When Reinsdorf bought the Bulls, Krause put in his bid. He told Reinsdorf: "Take a look at it for a year. If you don't like what you see, I'd like to talk to you about running that thing."

THE GRADUATE: Scottie Pippen holds aloft a copy of city's declaration that June 14 is Bulls Day in Chicago, while Mayor Daley shakes hands with John Paxson.
Photo by Nancy Stuenkel

Two weeks later, Reinsdorf interrupted one of Krause's baseball trips to the West Coast with the message: "Not a year. Now."

After the firing came the anointment.

Krause flew all night to get home and spent the next two days talking basketball with Reinsdorf before Thorn was fired and Krause anointed.

Krause looked at his players and was appalled. "We had a team that couldn't play together," he says now. "It took us two years to move the people we wanted to move out."

Only then could he begin serious rebuild-

I LOVE A PARADE: Fans offer congratulations to Stacey King and Dennis Hopson during the Bulls' victory parade.
Photo by Robert A. Davis

(Left) BRINGING HOME THE HARDWARE: Michael Jordan, between Scottie Pippen and coach Phil Jackson, exits the Bulls' plane with the Larry O'Brien Trophy, emblematic of the NBA champions. *Photo by Tom Cruze*

ing, with enough room under the NBA salary cap to make his moves.

"That first year was miserable," Krause painfully recalls. Jordan broke a foot. Many other Bulls were injured. Quintin Dailey was in and out of the drug tank. "I'd wake up nights and wonder, 'What's going to happen next?' " Krause said, while the news media were "rippin' me" because they couldn't understand, " 'Why'd Reinsdorf name him GM?' "

Krause traded his No. 1 draft choice, Keith Lee, and starting guard Ennis Whatley for an unknown power forward, Charles Oakley of Virginia Union, who would become the NBA's top rebounder. Rod Higgins was waived; David Greenwood, traded; Caldwell Jones, allowed to sign with Portland in exchange for a draft choice.

Paxson was first.

The first member of today's championship starting five to join Jordan was John Paxson, signed as a free agent from San Antonio. The Spurs were willing to waive right of first refusal for $200,000, a paltry sum by NBA standards.

Paxson was a point guard with accuracy from long range. "We had to get shooters around Jordan," Krause said. Every opponent would double- or triple-team Michael. He

FAN-TASTIC: Raucous fans celebrate during the rally in Grant Park that honored the NBA champion Bulls.
Photo by Al Podgorski

needed supplementary shooters who could exact a price for that over-play.

Then came Pippen and Grant.

Krause delayed his own progress with the unfortunate No. 1 choice of Brad Sellers in the 1986 draft. He recouped in 1987 with the draft that made a championship possible, using two first-round choices and astute trading to land Pippen and Horace Grant.

Marty Blake, the NBA director of scouting, had tipped Krause that a kid at little Central Arkansas, an NAIA school, was worth a look.

Krause first looked at Pippen in a tournament in Portsmouth, Va. Krause, who is short and fat, favors tall, gangly athletes with long arms. "Scottie's arms hung down to his knees," Krause gushed in remembrance. "I got that special feeling, that orgasm thing."

By draft day, Pippen was no secret. Everybody in the NBA knew he could play. Krause held the eighth and 10th picks in the first round, but now realized he would have to trade up to get Pippen. He rigged a deal involving future draft choices under which Seattle would take Pippen at No. 5 and swap him to the Bulls for Olden Polynice, whom the Bulls drafted at No. 8.

Krause was "stunned" to see Grant still available as his No. 10 pick approached. Had other NBA clubs noticed something wrong with Horace? Krause paced the floor outside the draft room in indecision.

Reinsdorf put his arm around him and said, "Go with your gut feeling."

Krause reminded himself he'd always gone for the "best available athlete." That clearly was Grant. So Horace was the pick.

Filling the hole in the middle.

With Grant as power forward of the future, Krause felt free to deal Oakley to fill the hole at center.

With Jordan on the team, Krause realized, the Bulls never would be so bad they would qualify for the lottery pick necessary to draft a Hakeem Olajuwon or David Robinson.

Krause wanted not one, but two centers: a veteran who could fill the role for a few seasons and a rookie with the potential to be useful after a few seasons of hard grooming.

Using Oakley as bait, Krause got the New York Knicks to give him Bill Cartwright and a switch of first-round choices that allowed him to take Will Perdue.

The deal was risky and wildly unpopular in Chicago. A fine young player, Oakley, was being sacrificed. Cartwright had a reputation as a chronic injury case with bad feet. At first sight, Perdue looked clumsy as a newborn giraffe.

Krause brought Cartwright in for a thorough physical before making the deal and was convinced Cartwright was sound. But Cartwright did not readily adapt to the Bulls' offense, and Perdue seemed a useless stiff.

Cartwright lost time to injuries last season. He needed postseason surgery to loosen knees he couldn't even bend in the playoffs last spring. With limber knees, he became the force this season Krause had always advertised he

MOB SCENE: An estimated 300,000 fans filled Grant Park to cheer their heroes one more time. *Photo by Tom Cruze*

'BEST WISHES'. . .Michael Jordan pleases a young fan with an autograph.
Photo by Bob Ringham

(Left) BULL FIGHTER: A surprised fan tries to escape the clutches of Benny the Bull.
Photo by Robert A. Davis

would be. He neutralized opposing centers in the playoffs.

Perdue, meanwhile, blossomed under the tutelage of coaches Phil Jackson and Tex Winter and strength coach Al Vermeil, becoming Cartwright's productive sub.

Today's starting lineup was intact in 1989. Why did it take so long to win? Pippen and Grant needed to grow, Cartwright had to blend. Reserve strength had to be fortified by the development of Perdue and B. J. Armstrong and the acquisition of Cliff Levingston.

The controversial coaching change.

And, according to Krause and Reinsdorf, there had to be a coaching change a lot of us criticized.

Krause dumped the popular and charismatic Doug Collins and settled on Jackson, less showy but more serene.

Krause felt the fatherly Jackson would be better than Collins at grooming young players and stroking their psyches. Jackson had played under Red Holzman, the legendary Knicks coach whom Reinsdorf revered.

Jackson and assistant John Bach installed the defenses that frustrated Bulls opponents through these playoffs.

It was a gambling pressure system involving rapid double-teams and rotations. It worked so well, according to Detroit coach Chuck Daly and Lakers coach Mike Dunleavy, because the Bulls had such outstanding athletic ability in Jordan, Pippen and Grant.

But Jackson says the vital part was Paxson. Paxson isn't especially quick or fast, but he was the only Bulls guard "who felt comfortable getting up-court and turning (opposing) point guards," Jackson said. "When John exhibited the desire and tenacity to put pressure on the ball, I knew he would have to start."

Finally, there was the tricky diplomatic chore. Jackson had to convince Jordan, the greatest scorer in the sport, to spread the basketball around to a supporting cast that now was able to make good use of it.

Jordan still led the league in scoring, but his deft passes brought other Bulls into production and confounded opposing defenses. He earned his MVP trophy in all phases of the game.

Going into the playoffs, there was a feeling around the NBA the best teams were in the West, especially in Portland. The notion was the Bulls had been lucky winners in an Eastern Conference weakened by injuries to Detroit, Boston, Cleveland and Philadelphia.

The day before the last game in Los Angeles, a Western sportswriter suggested to Dunleavy, the Lakers' coach, his team had beaten the league's best in Portland during the semifinals.

"I don't think so," Dunleavy replied. "The team we're playing now is the best we've faced."

The word "team" did not fit Jordan & Company until this season. Only by becoming a team did they become fit to be Chicago's first NBA champions.

(Next page) WHAT IT'S ALL ABOUT: Michael Jordan holds aloft the championship trophy after addressing fans who showed up at the airport to greet the conquering heroes. *Photo by Jon Sall*

WHOA: Scottie Pippen lends a restraining hand to the New York Knicks' Maurice Cheeks during the Bulls' triumphant play-off series. *Photo by Robert A. Davis*

ONE MORE WIN: Scottie Pippen (left), Horace Grant and Michael Jordan start to share some high fives with John Paxson waiting in the background. *Photo by Robert A. Davis*

SO LITTLE TIME: Michael Jordan checks the scoreboard at foul line during the final play-off game with the Los Angeles Lakers in Los Angeles. *Photo by Robert A. Davis*

6

The Statistics

The Bulls '90-91 Game By Game

REGULAR SEASON

GAME	DATE	OPPONENT	W/L	BULLS-OPP	RECORD	HIGH SCORER
1	11/02	Philadelphia	L	116-124	0-1	Jordan (34)
2	11/03	Washington	L	102-103	0-2	Jordan (28)
3	11/06	Boston	L	108-110	0-3	Jordan (33)
4	11/07	Minnesota	W	96-91	1-3	Jordan (17)
5	11/09	Boston	W	120-100	2-3	Jordan (41)
6	11/10	Charlotte	W	105-86	3-3	Jordan (23)
7	11/12	Utah	W	84-82	4-3	Jordan (29)
8	11/15	Holden State	L	93-103	4-4	Grant (18)
9	11/17	Seattle	W	11695	5-4	Jordan (33)
10	11/18	Portland	L	112-125	5-5	Jordan (29)
11	11/21	Phoenix	L	107-109	5-6	Jordan (34)
12	11/23	La Clippers	W	105-97	6-6	Paxson (26)
13	11/24	Denver	W	151-145	7-6	Jordan (38)
14	11/28	Washington	W	118-94	8-6	Jordan (24)
15	11/30	Indiana	W	124-95	9-6	Jordan (37)
16	12/01	Cleveland	W	120-85	10-6	Jordan (32)
17	12/04	Phoenix	W	155-127	11-6	Jordan (27)
18	12/07	New York	W	108-98	12-6	Jordan (33)
19	12/08	Portland	L	101-109	12-7	Jordan (35)
20	12/11	Milwaukee	L	87-99	12-8	Jordan (31)
21	12/14	LA Clippers	W	128-88	13-8	Pippen (22)
22	12/15	Cleveland	W	11698	14-8	Jordan (24)
23	12/18	Miami	W	112-103	15-8	Jordan (39)
24	12/19	Detroit	L	84-105	15-9	Jordan (33)
25	12/21	La Lakers	W	114-103	169	Jordan (33)
26	12/22	Indiana	W	128-118	17-9	Jordan (29)
27	12/25	Detroit	W	98-86	18-9	Jordan (37)
28	12/27	Golden State	W	128-113	19-9	Jordan (42)
29	12/29	Seattle	W	116-91	20-9	Jordan (31)
30	1/03	Houston	L	92-114	20-10	Jordan (32)
31	1/05	Cleveland	W	108-92	21-10	Jordan (30)
32	1/08	New Jersey	W	111-102	22-10	Jordan (41)
33	1/09	Philadelphia	W	107-99	23-10	Jordan (40)
34	1/11	Atlanta	W	99-96	24-10	Jordan (31)
35	1/12	Charlotte	W	106-95	25-10	Jordan (33)
36	1/14	Milwaukee	W	110-97	26-13	Jordan (34)
37	1/16	Orlando	W	99-88	27-10	Jordan (29)
38	1/18	Atlanta	L	105-114	27-11	Jordan (30)
39	1/21	Miami	W	117-106	28-11	Jordan (37)
40	1/23	New Jersey	L	95-99	28-12	Jordan (35)
41	1/25	Miami	W	108-87	29-12	Jordan (26)
42	1/31	San Antonio	L	102-106	29-13	Jordan (36)
43	2/1	Dallas	W	101-90	30-13	Jordan (31)
44	2/3	La Lakers	L	86-99	30-14	Pippen (24)
45	2/4	Sacramento	W	108-97	31-14	Jordan (24)
46	2/7	Detroit	W	95-93	32-14	Jordan (30)
47	2/12	Atlanta	W	122-113	33-14	Jordan (32)
48	2/14	New York	W	102-92	34-14	Jordan (29)
49	2/16	New Jersey	W	99-87	35-14	Jordan (26)
50	2/18	Cleveland	W	110-95	36-14	Jordan (32)
51	2/19	Washington	W	118-113	37-14	Jordan (40)
52	2/22	Sacramento	W	129-82	38-14	Jordan (34)
53	2/23	Charlotte	W	129-108	39-14	Pippen (43)
54	2/26	Boston	W	129-99	40-14	Jordan (39)

The Bulls '90-91
Game By Game cont'd

55	3/1	Dallas	W	109-86	41-14	Jordan (29)
56	3/2	Indiana	L	114-135	41-15	Jordan (22)
57	3/5	Milwaukee	W	104-86	42-15	Jordan (30)
58	3/8	Utah	W	99-89	43-15	Jordan (37)
59	3/10	Atlanta	W	122-87	44-15	Jordan (25)
60	3/12	Minnesota	W	131-99	45-15	Jordan (20)
61	3/13	Milwaukee	W	102-101	46-15	Jordan (39)
62	3/15	Charlotte	W	105-92	47-15	Jordan (34)
63	3/16	Cleveland	W	102-98	48-15	Jordan (37)
64	3/18	Denver	W	121-108	49-15	Jordan (31)
65	3/20	Atlanta	W	129-107	50-15	Jordan (22)
66	3/22	Philadelphia	L	90-95	50-16	Jordan (20)
67	3/23	Indiana	W	133-119	51-16	Jordan (39)
68	3/25	Houston	L	90-100	51-17	Jordan (34)
69	3/28	New Jersey	W	128-94	52-17	Jordan (42)
70	3/29	Washington	W	112-94	53-17	Grant (22) Pippen (22)
71	3/31	Boston	L	132-135	53-18	Jordan (37)
72	4/2	Orlando	W	106-102	54-18	Jordan (44)
73	4/4	New York	W	101-91	55-18	Jordan (34)
74	4/5	San Antonio	L	107-110	55-19	Jordan (39)
75	4/7	Philadelphia	L	111-114	55-20	Jordan (41)
76	4/9	New York	W	108-106	56-20	Jordan (28)
77	4/10	Indiana	W	101-96	57-20	Jordan (28)
78	4/12	Detroit	L	91-95	57-21	Jordan (40)
79	4/15	Milwaukee	W	103-94	58-21	Jordan (46)
80	4/17	Miami	W	111-101	59-21	Jordan (26)
81	4/19	Charlotte	W	115-99	60-21	Jordan (41)
82	4/21	Detroit	W	108-100	61-21	Pippen (28)

PLAYOFFS

1	4/25	New York	W	126-85	1-0	Jordan (28)
2	4/28	New York	W	89-79	2-0	Jordan (26)
3	4/30	New York	W	103-94	3-0	Jordan (33)
4	5/4	Philadelphia	W	105-92	1-0	Jordan (29)
6	5/6	Philadelphia	W	112-100	2-0	Jordan (29)
7	5/10	Phildelphia	L	97-99	2-1	Jordan (46)
8	5/12	Philadelphia	W	101-85	3-1	Jordan (25)
9	5/14	Philadelphia	W	100-95	4-1	Jordan (38)
10	5/19	Detroit	W	94-83	1-0	Jordan (22)
11	5/21	Detroit	W	105-97	2-0	Jordan (35)
12	5/25	Detroit	W	113-107	3-0	Jordan (33)
13	5/27	Detroit	W	115-94	4-0	Jordan (29)
14	6/2	Los Angeles	L	91-93	0-1	Jordan (36)
15	6/5	Los Angeles	W	107-86	1-1	Jordan (33)
16	6/7	Los Angeles	W	104-96	2-1	Jordan (29)
17	6/9	Los Angeles	W	97-82	3-1	Jordan (28)
18	6/12	Los Angeles	W	108-101	4-1	Pippen (32)

NBA Finals boxes

GAME 1
Lakers 93, Bulls 91

Lakers	29	22	24	18—93
BULLS	30	23	15	23—91

LAKERS	MIN	FG-FGA	FT-A	R	A	PF	TP
James Worthy, f	45	11-24	0-0	3	1	2	22
Sam Perkins, f	40	8-17	3-6	4	0	1	22
Vlade Divac, c	44	5-11	6-6	14	1	4	16
Byron Scott, g	37	1-4	7-8	2	2	4	9
Magic Johnson, g	43	4-5	9-10	10	11	2	19
A.C. Green	16	0-1	3-4	3	0	0	3
Terry Teagle	10	1-3	0-0	1	0	1	2
Larry Drew	5	0-1	0-0	0	0	2	0
Totals	240	30-66	28-34	37	15	16	93

- Percentages—FG .455, FT .824.
- 3-point goals—5-10, .500 (Johnson 2-2, Perkins 3-4, Worthy 0-2, Scott 0-1, Drew 0-1).
- Team rebounds—6.
- Blocked shots—3 (Divac).
- Turnovers—13, (Johnson 5, Divac 4, Worthy 2, Perkins, Teagle).
- Steals—7 (Divac 3, Perkins, Worthy, Scott, Johnson).

BULLS	MIN	FG-FGA	FT-A	R	A	PF	TP
Scottie Pippen, f	41	7-19	5-7	7	5	5	19
Horace Grant, f	40	3-8	0-0	10	1	1	6
Bill Cartwright, c	34	3-8	0-0	4	2	4	6
John Paxson, g	30	3-7	0-0	4	2	4	6
Michael Jordan, g	40	14-24	7-9	8	12	5	36
Will Perdue	12	2-2	2-2	4	0	2	6
Cliff Levingston	20	1-2	0-0	2	1	0	2
B.J. Armstrong	10	3-5	0-0	3	2		6
Craig Hodges	13	2-5	0-0	0	0	0	4
Totals	240	38-80	14-18	39	26	21	91

- Percentages—FG .475, FT .788.
- 3-point goals—1-7, .143 (Jordan 1-1, Pippen 0-2, Hodges 0-2, Paxson 0-1, Armstrong 0-1).
- Team rebounds—6.
- Blocked shots—5 (Pippen 2, Cartwright, Levingston, Perdue).
- Turnovers—10 (Jordan 4, Pippen 3, Grant Hodges, Levingston).
- Steals—11 (Jordan 3, Grant 2, Paxson 2, Levingston 2, Pippen, Armstrong).

- Officials—Hugh Evans, Hue Hollins, Jack Madden.
- Attendance—18,676.

GAME 2
Bulls 107, Lakers 86

L.A. Lakers	23	20	26	17— 86
Bulls	28	20	38	21— 107

LAKERS	MIN	FG-FGA	FT-A	R	A	PF	TP
Sam Perkins, f	35	4-8	2-2	6	0	2	11
James Worthy, f	40	9-17	5-6	1	1	3	24
Vlade Divac, c	41	7-11	2-2	5	5	2	16
Byron Scott, g	26	2-2	0-0	0	2	4	5
Magic Johnson, g	43	4-13	6-6	7	10	2	14
Mych. Thompson	10	0-3	0-0	0	0	1	0
A.C. Green	22	2-11	0-0	7	0	2	6
Terry Teagle	14	0-2	6-6	1	1	1	6
Larry Drew	5	2-4	0-0	1	0	0	4
Elden Campbell	4	0-2	0-0	2	0	0	0
Totals	240	30-73	21-22	34	19	15	86

- Percentages—FG .411, FT .955.
- 3-point goals—5-12, .417 (Green 2-3, Scott 1-1, Perkins 1-2, Worthy 1-2, Divac 0-1, Drew 0-1, Johnson 0-2).
- Team rebounds—5.
- Blocked shots—2 (Divac, Campbell).
- Turnovers—17 (Worthy 4, Johnson 4, Perkins 3, Divac 2, Teagle 2, Thompson, Campbell).
- Steals—8 (Divac 3, Johnson 2, Scott, Green, Campbell).
- Technical fouls—Illegal defense, 9:40 fourth.
- Flagrant fouls—Scott, 8:05 third.
- Illegal defense—1.

BULLS	MIN	FG-FGA	FT-A	R	A	PF	TP
Scott Pippen, f	44	8-16	4-4	5	10	4	20
Horace Grant, f	40	10-13	0-0	5	1	1	20
Bill Cartwright, c	24	6-9	0-0	5	1	1	12
John Paxson, g	25	8-8	0-0	0	6	2	16
Michael Jordan, g	36	15-18	3-4	7	13	4	33
Cliff Levingston	22	0-2	0-0	1	2	4	0
Craig Hodges	11	1-6	0-0	1	0	1	2
Will Perdue	11	1-3	0-0	7	1	0	2
B.J. Armstrong	7	0-2	0-0	1	1	0	0
Scott Williams	15	1-1	0-0	3	0	2	2
Stacey King	3	0-3	0-0	1	0	1	0
Dennis Hopson	2	0-0	0-0	0	0	0	0
Totals	240	50-81	7-8	36	35	20	107

- Percentages—FG .617, FT .875.
- 3-point goals—0-5, .000 (King 0-1, Jordan 0-1, Hodges 0-3).
- Team rebounds—1.
- Blocked shots—1 (Jordan).
- Turnovers—14 (Pippen 5, Jordan 4, Cartwright 2, Grant, Perdue, King).
- Steals—10 (Grant 2, Cartwright 2, Jordan 2, Levingston 2, Pippen, Paxson).
- Technical fouls—None.
- Illegal defense—1.

- Officials—Jess Kersey, Mike Mathis, Jake O'Donnell.
- A—18,676. T—2:10.

GAME 3
Bulls 104, Lakers 96

BULLS	25	23	18	26	12—104
Lakers	25	22	25	20	4—96

BULLS	MIN	FG-FGA	FT-A	R	A	PF	TP
Horace Grant, f	42	9-11	4-4	11	3	2	22
Scottie Pippen, f	45	8-17	3-4	13	5	6	19
Bill Cartwright, c	33	2-8	2-2	3	1	3	6
Michael Jordan, g	52	11-28	6-6	9	9	5	29
John Paxson, g	36	5-11	0-0	3	1	0	10
Will Perdue	6	0-0	0-0	1	0	1	0
Craig Hodges	8	1-3	0-0	1	0	0	2
Cliff Levingston	20	5-5	0-0	4	0	1	10
B.J. Armstrong	9	0-1	0-0	0	0	0	0
Scott Williams	11	0-1	4-6	2	2	1	4
Stacey King	3	0-0	2-2	0	0	1	2
Totals	265	41-85	21-24	46	23	21	104

- Percentages: FG .482, FT .875.
- 3-Point Goals—1-3, .333 (Jordan 1-1, Pippen 0-1, Paxson 0-1).
- Team Rebounds: 11.
- Blocked shots: 5 (Levingston 3, Jordan 2).
- Turnovers: 16 (Grant 5, Cartwright 4, Pippen 3, Jordan 3, Perdue).
- Steals: 10 (Pippen 4, Jordan 4, Grant, Levingston).
- Technical fouls: Pippen, :31 second.
- Illegal defense: None.

LAKERS	MIN	FG-FGA	FT-A	R	A	PF	TP
Sam Perkins, f	51	10-17	5-6	9	2	3	25
James Worthy, f	48	9-16	1-2	1	4	1	19
Vlade Divac, c	41	11-15	2-2	7	0	6	24
Magic Johnson, g	50	7-15	8-9	6	10	2	22
Byron Scott, g	43	0-8	0-2	1	3	3	0
Terry Teagle	11	1-2	0-2	0	2	0	2
A.C. Green	15	1-3	0-2	4	0	2	2
Larry Drew	4	0-1	0-0	1	0	0	0
Elden Campbell	2	1-2	0-0	0	0	1	2
Totals	265	40-79	16-25	29	19	20	96

- Percentages: FG .506, FT .640.
- 3-Point Goals: 0-8, .000 (Drew 0-1, Worthy 0-2, Johnson 0-2, Scott 0-3).
- Team Rebounds: 9.
- Blocked shots: 7 (Perkins 5, Divac, Teagle).
- Turnovers: 14 (Johnson 5, Perkins 3, Divac 2, Scott 2, Worthy, Green).
- Steals: 9 (Worthy 3, Divac 2, Johnson 2, Perkins, Teagle).
- Technical fouls: None.
- Illegal defense: None.

- Officials—Darell Garretson, Bill Oakes, Joe Crawford.
- A—17,505.

BULLS							
				27 25 22 23	—	97
Lakers				28 16 14 24	—	82

BULLS	MIN	FG-FGA	FT-A	R	A	PF	TP
Scottie Pippen, f	40	6-12	2-2	9	6	4	14
Horace Grant, f	36	6-14	2-2	7	3	3	14
Bill Cartwright, c	36	5-10	2-4	5	1	1	12
John Paxson, g	35	7-11	0-0	3	2	1	15
Michael Jordan, g	44	11-20	6-6	5	13	3	28
Will Perdue	1	0-0	0-0	0	0	0	0
Cliff Levingston	20	2-3	0-0	5	0	3	4
B.J. Armstrong	3	1-1	0-0	0	0	0	2
Craig Hodges	14	3-7	0-0	1	1	3	6
Scott Williams	11	1-2	0-0	3	1	4	2
Dennis Hopson							DNP
Stacey King							DNP
Totals	240	42-80	12-14	38	27	22	97

■ Percentages—FG .525, FT .857.
■ 3-point goals—1-3, .333 (Paxson 1-2, Jordan 0-1).
■ Team rebounds—6.
■ Blocked shots—8 (Pippen 2, Cartwright 2, Jordan 2, Grant, Levingston).
■ Turnovers—5 (Pippen 2, Jordan, Paxson, Hodges).
■ Steals—4 (Grant 2, Pippen, Paxson).

LAKERS	MIN	FG-FGA	FT-A	R	A	PF	TP
Sam Perkins, f	43	1-15	1-2	10	0	5	3
James Worthy, f	31	6-16	0-1	3	2	2	12
Vlade Divac, c	45	12-20	3-1	11	1	4	27
Magic Johnson, g	44	6-13	10-10	6	11	4	22
Byron Scott, g	34	2-4	0-0	4	0	5	4
A.C. Green	17	1-5	3-4	7	0	1	5
Terry Teagle	18	1-6	4-4	0	1	6
Larry Drew	6	1-2	1-2	0	0	1	3
Tony Smith	2	0-1	0-0	1	0	0	0
Elden Campbell							DNP
M. Thompson							DNP
Irving Thomas							DNP
Totals	240	30-82	22-16	42	14	23	82

■ Percentages—FG .366, FT .846.
■ 3-point goals—0-5, .000 (Johnson 0-2, Perkins 0-3).
■ Team rebounds—10.
■ Blocked shots—3 (Divac 3).
■ Turnovers—9 (Divac 2, Johnson 2, Scott 2, Green 2, Smith).
■ Steals—4 (Teagle 2, Divac, Scott).

■ Officials—Hugh Evans, Ed T. Rush, Dick Bavetta.
■ Attendance—17,505.

Bulls					
Bulls		27 21 32	28—108
L.A. Lakers		25 24 31	21—101

BULLS	MIN	FG-FGA	FT-FTA	R	A	PF	TP
Horace Grant, f	40	4-5	3-6	6	0	2	11
Scottie Pippen, f	48	10-22	11-12	13	7	3	32
Bill Cartwright, c	33	4-11	0-0	8	7	5	8
Michael Jordan, g	48	12-23	6-8	4	10	1	30
John Paxson, g	33	9-12	2-2	3	4	3	20
Cliff Levingston	8	0-1	0-0	2	0	4	0
Craig Hodges	7	2-2	0-0	0	0	0	5
Scott Williams	8	0-0	0-0	1	0	2	0
B.J. Armstrong	8	1-2	0-0	0	0	0	2
Will Perdue	7	0-0	0-0	0	0	3	0
Stacey King	dnp						
Dennis Hopson	dnp						
Totals	240	42-78	22-28	37	28	23	108

■ Percentages—FG .538, FT .786.
■ 3-point goals—2-3, .667 (Hodges 1-1, Pippen 1-2).
■ Team rebounds—6.
■ Blocked shots—6 (Grant 2, Jordan 2, Pippen, Williams).
■ Turnovers—18 (Pippen 7, Jordan 6, Grant 2, Paxson, Armstrong, Perdue).
■ Steals—14 (Jordan 5, Pippen 5, Grant, Cartwright, Paxson, Armstrong).
■ Technical fouls—None.

LAKERS	MIN	FG-FGA	FT-FTA	R	A	PF	TP
A.C. Green, f	43	6-12	1-2	7	1	3	13
Sam Perkins, f	37	5-12	11-13	9	3	4	22
Vlade Divac, c	37	4-12	0-0	7	3	2	8
Magic Johnson, g	48	4-12	6-6	11	20	0	16
Terry Teagle, g	18	4-8	1-2	0	0	4	9
Elden Campbell	27	9-12	3-4	2	0	3	21
Tony Smith	30	5-6	2-3	0	2	6	12
James Worthy	dnp						
Byron Scott	dnp						
Larry Drew	dnp						
M. Thompson	dnp						
Irving Thomas	dnp						
Totals	240	37-74	24-30	36	29	22	101

■ Percentages—FG .500, FT .800.
■ 3-point goals—3-11, .273 (Johnson 2-6, Perkins 1-4, Divac 0-1).
■ Team rebounds—6.
■ Blocked shots—7 (Divac 4, Perkins 2, Campbell).
■ Turnovers—22 (Johnson 6, Divac 5, Smith 4, Teagle 3, Green 2, Perkins, Campbell).
■ Steals—6 (Green 2, Campbell 2, Johnson, Smith).
■ Technical fouls—None.
■ Flagrant fouls—Perkins, 7:43 fourth.

■ Officials—Jake O'Donnell, Jack Madden, Mike Mathis.
■ A—17,505. T—2:28.

B.J. ARMSTRONG

■ **Position:** Guard. **Height:** 6-2. **Weight:** 175. **Age:** 23.
■ **College:** Iowa '89.
■ **Acquired:** Bulls' second first-round draft choice in 1989 (18th overall).
■ **1990-91:** Played off the bench in all 82 games. Scored season-high 19 points in back-to-back games on March 10 at Atlanta and March 12 vs. Minnesota. Best month of the season was March when he averaged 11.1 ppg, 4.3 apg and shot 54 percent from the field (83-154) and 54 percent from three-point range (7-13). Averaged 8.8 ppg and 3.7 apg (third on team).
■ **Comment:** Far surpassed Stacey King as the best second-year player on the Bulls. His boyish good looks make him a fan favorite. An off-season weightlifting program helped prepare him for NBA grind. Ability to run point and hit open jumper has attracted trade interest.

BILL CARTWRIGHT

■ **Position:** Center. **Height:** 7-1. **Weight:** 245. **Age:** 34.
■ **College:** University of San Francisco '79.
■ **Acquired:** Traded to Chicago with the 1988 No. 11 draft pick overall (Will Perdue) from the New York Knicks on June 27, 1988, for Charles Oakley and the No. 16 pick in 1988.
■ **1990-91:** Started 79 games this year. Best month of the season was December when he averaged 11.2 ppg and 7.5 rpg. Had a six-game streak of double figures scoring from Dec. 21 and Jan. 3. Averaged 9.6 ppg and 6.2 rpg this year.
■ **Comment:** Became mired in controversy when a stray elbow in early January put Hakeem Olajuwon on the sidelines for two months. NBA operations director Rod Thorn ordered him to wear elbow pads, but Cartwright refused and got away with it. Competent, not dominant.

HORACE GRANT

■ **Position:** Forward. **Height:** 6-10. **Weight:** 220. **Age:** 25.
■ **College:** Clemson '87.
■ **Acquired:** Bulls' first-round pick in '87 (10th overall).
■ **1990-91:** Played in 82 games this season. Tied his career-high 25 points vs. Phoenix on Dec. 4. Tied his career-high for rebounds when he had 18 in the March 31 game at Boston. Led team in rebounding this season with an 8.4 average and ranked third on the team in scoring with a 12.8 average. Best month was March when he averaged 14.9 ppg and 10.1 rpg. and shot 55 percent from the field (83-150).
■ **Comment:** The goggled wonder was the team's unsung hero, especially vs. LA. After a trip to the opthamologist revealed nearsightedness, Grant wore an assortment of eyewear, turning to a pair of clear goggles in the second game of the Lakers series.

STACEY KING

■ **Position:** Center. **Height:** 6-11. **Weight:** 230. **Age:** 24.
■ **College:** Oklahoma '89.
■ **Acquired:** Bulls' first pick in '89 draft (6th overall).
■ **1990-91:** In his second NBA season, played in 76 games. The Bulls went 5-1 when Stacey started this season. Was suspended by the team from the April 2 game against Orlando after he walked out on a practice the previous day. His best month was December when he averaged 7.0 points. Scored in double figures 11 times. Scored his season-high 16 points on Feb. 4 at Sacramento.
■ **Comment:** Somewhere along the line Sky King became Burger King. Upset over playing time and criticism, he left the Deerfield Multiplex before practice on April 1 and was suspended one game. Lost his WMAQ-TV television gig.

CLIFF LEVINGSTON

■ **Position:** Forward. **Height:** 6-8. **Weight:** 210. **Age:** 30.
■ **College:** Wichita State '83.
■ **Acquired:** Signed as unrestricted free agent Oct. 4, 1990.
■ **1990-91:** In his Bulls debut on opening night, he scored eight points and grabbed a team-high six rebounds. Had his best month of the season in November, averaging 5.1 points, 4.8 rebounds and 15.6 minutes. Led the Bulls in rebounds four times. Had his season-high 14 points on March 10 at Atlanta and grabbed his season-high 12 rebounds on Nov. 9 at Boston.
■ **Comment:** The Good News was delivered in the playoffs, particularly against the Pistons and Lakers. Struggled to contribute during the season, but completely redeemed himself with great playoff, especially against Lakers. Tough on the boards and great defensively.

JOHN PAXSON

■ **Position:** Guard. **Height:** 6-2. **Weight:** 185. **Age:** 30.
■ **College:** Notre Dame '83.
■ **Acquired:** Signed as a free agent Oct. 30, 1985.
■ **1990-91:** Started every game this season. Scored his career-high 28 points at Boston on March 31. Scored in double figures 30 times. Scored 20 or more four times. Led the team in assists eight times. Best month was March when he averaged 9.9 ppg and shot 56 percent from the field (78-140). Ranked 10th in the league in field-goal percentage at .548 (317-578). Longest double-figure scoring streak was four games.
■ **Comment:** The most underpaid player in the NBA at $325,000, this unrestricted free agent should reap a big pay day. Proved his worth in Lakers series when he connected on 32-of-49 shots, including 5-for-5 down the stretch in the deciding game.

NBA championship this year

CRAIG HODGES

- **Position:** Guard. **Height:** 6-2. **Weight:** 190. **Age:** 30.
- **College:** Long Beach State '82.
- **Acquired:** Traded by Phoenix for Ed Nealy and a 1989 draft pick on Dec. 14. 1988.
- **1990-91:** Came off bench in 73 games this season. Averaged 5.0 ppg. Went 44-115 (.383) from three-point range. Won his second consecutive three-point championship at All-Star weekend in February. Made 19 straight three-pointers during a qualifying round. His best month was February when he averaged 6.3 points and shot 44 percent from three-point range (7-16).
- **Comment:** The trigger-happy trey-ster proved to be a streak shooter completely without conscience when it comes to launching a long-range jumper. Highlight of his season was leading team in Lord's Prayer following NBA title victory.

DENNIS HOPSON

- **Position:** Guard. **Height:** 6-5. **Weight:** 200. **Age:** 26.
- **College:** Ohio State '87.
- **Acquired:** Traded by the New Jersey Nets on June 26, 1990, for the Bulls' 1990 first-round pick (Tate George) and second-round picks in '91 and '92.
- **1990-91:** Scored nine points, grabbed five rebounds and had one steal in his Bulls debut vs. Philadelphia on Nov. 2. Played 61 games this season, all off the bench. Averaged 4.3 ppg and 11.9 mpg. Scored season-high 14 points on Dec. 15 vs. Cleveland. Best month was November, when he averaged 5.7 ppg and 14.5 mpg.
- **Comment:** Wept in locker room following sweep of Detroit because he felt he hadn't contributed. Never seemed to get into sync this season due to some nagging injuries. He stubbed a toe in early February and appeared in just 16 games the rest of the way.

MICHAEL JORDAN

- **Position:** Guard. **Height:** 6-6. **Weight:** 198. **Age:** 28.
- **College:** North Carolina '85.
- **Acquired:** Bulls' first choice in '84 (third overall).
- **1990-91:** Led the league in scoring for the fifth straight year with a 31.5 average. Scored his 15,000th point at Philadelphia on Jan. 9. Scored season-high 46 points vs. Milwaukee April 15. Scored 30 or more points 52 times, scored 40 or more points in 11 games. Member of the 1991 All-Star team and leading vote-getter. Was NBA Player of the Week twice this season and Player of the Month for March.
- **Comment:** Everybody's MVP. For all his dunks, twisting layups, long jumpers and great defensive plays, Jordan's best moment may have come in the locker room. With his father on one side and his wife on the other, he wept as he held the championship trophy.

WILL PERDUE

- **Position:** Center. **Height:** 7-0. **Weight:** 240. **Age:** 25.
- **College:** Vanderbilt '88.
- **Acquired:** Bulls first pick in '88 draft (11th overall).
- **1990-91:** Played in 74 games. Had three double-doubles in scoring and rebounding this season. Grabbed his career-high 14 rebounds at Sacramento on Feb. 4. Scored his career-high 15 points vs. Detroit on April 21. Scored in double figures eight times. Best month was March when he averaged 4.6 points, 5.9 rebounds, 16.1 minutes and shot 53 percent from the field (34-64) in 17 games. Led the team in rebounds nine times.
- **Comment:** Once the favorite of Stadium boobirds, Perdue became a crowd favorite with tremendous playoff performances against New York, Philadelphia and Detroit. A legitimate NBA backup center who might be ready to start.

SCOTTIE PIPPEN

- **Position:** Guard. **Height:** 6-7. **Weight:** 210. **Age:** 25.
- **College:** Central Arkansas '87.
- **Acquired:** Draft rights, No. 5 overall, traded by Seattle to Bulls on June 22, 1987, for draft rights to Olden Polynice, plus a second-round pick.
- **1990-91:** Started all 82 games. Had a career-high 15 assists vs. Indiana on Nov. 30. Scored career-high 43 points vs. Charlotte on Feb. 23. Team leader in assists (6.2) and blocks (1.13), ranked second in scoring (17.8), rebounds (7.3) and steals (2.35). Best month was February when he averaged 21.2 ppg and 7.7 rpg.
- **Comment:** The season Pippen left every ghost of playoffs past behind. Produced career highs in scoring and rebounding while emerging as one of the NBA's premier players. Only dark spot on season was public airing of contract dispute.

SCOTT WILLIAMS

- **Position:** Center. **Height:** 6-10. **Weight:** 230. **Age:** 22.
- **College:** North Carolina '90.
- **Acquired:** Signed as free agent July 25, 1990.
- **1990-91:** Only rookie on the Bulls. Made his NBA debut on opening night when he played two scoreless minutes vs. Philadelphia but had one rebound. The next night at Washington, he scored his first NBA points when he had five, along with season-high seven rebounds. Scored season-high 10 points at Denver on Nov. 24. Best month was December when he played in eight games and averaged 3.8 points and 2.3 rebounds.
- **Comment:** A surprise contributor, Williams got plenty of quality minutes in the Lakers series. If chronic shoulder problems can be solved could be a part of this team for a long time. A favorite of Jordan, who seems to love everyone from North Carolina.

Bulls playoff statistics

Player	G	Avg Min	FG M-A	FG Pct	3-Pt M-A	FT M-A	FT Pct	Pts	Avg	HG
Jordan	17	40.5	197-376	.524	10-26	125-148	.845	529	31.1	46
Pippen	17	41.4	142-282	.504	4-17	80-101	.792	368	21.6	32
Grant	17	39.2	91-156	.583	0-0	44-60	.733	226	13.3	22
Cartwright	17	30.1	70-135	.519	0-0	22-32	.688	162	9.5	16
Paxson	17	28.6	62-117	.530	2-14	14-14	1.000	140	8.2	20
Armstrong	17	16.1	35-70	.500	3-5	20-25	.800	93	5.5	18
Hodges	17	12.3	33-78	.423	11-28	3-4	.750	80	4.7	16
Perdue	17	11.6	29-53	.547	0-0	12-22	.545	70	4.1	16
Levingston	17	11.3	21-41	.512	0-0	3-6	.500	45	2.6	10
King	11	7.8	8-27	.296	0-1	7-11	.636	23	2.1	4
Williams	12	6.0	6-13	.462	0-1	11-20	.550	23	1.9	5
Hopson	5	3.6	2-6	.333	0-0	4-9	.444	8	1.6	3
Team	17	241.5	696-1354	.514	30-92	345-452	.763	1767	103.9	126
Opponents	17	241.5	574-1275	.450	50-152	370-461	.803	1568	92.2	107

Player	Off Reb	Def Reb	Tot Reb	Reb Avg	Ast	Ast Avg	PF	FO	Stl	To	Blk
Jordan	18	90	108	6.4	142	8.4	53	0	40	43	23
Pippen	37	114	151	8.9	99	5.8	58	1	42	55	19
Grant	56	82	138	8.1	38	2.2	45	0	15	20	6
Cartwright	25	55	80	4.7	32	1.9	55	0	9	21	7
Paxson	2	21	23	1.4	53	3.1	32	0	11	6	0
Armstrong	5	22	27	1.6	43	2.5	13	0	19	13	1
Hodges	0	4	4	0.2	10	0.6	21	0	11	11	0
Perdue	32	33	65	3.8	4	0.2	41	1	2	14	8
Levingston	22	19	41	2.4	7	0.4	28	0	10	2	7
King	9	13	22	2.0	2	0.2	15	0	1	9	1
Williams	4	16	20	1.7	3	0.3	15	0	1	4	3
Hopson	2	2	4	0.8	1	0.2	2	0	0	1	1
Team	212	471	683	40.2	434	25.5	378	2	161	212	76
Opponents	198	413	611	35.9	327	19.2	398	5	115	270	65

Bulls regular season statistics

Player	G	Avg Min	FG M-A	FG Pct	3-Pt M-A	FT M-A	FT Pct	Pts	Avg	HG
Jordan	82	37.0	990-1837	.539	29-93	571-671	.851	2580	31.5	46
Pippen	82	36.8	600-1153	.520	21-68	240-340	.706	1461	17.8	43
Grant	78	33.9	401-733	.547	1-6	197-277	.711	1000	12.8	25
Cartwright	79	28.8	318-649	.490	0-0	124-178	.697	760	9.6	20
Armstrong	82	21.1	304-632	.481	15-30	97-111	.874	720	8.8	19
Paxson	82	24.0	317-578	.548	42-96	34-41	.829	710	8.7	28
King	76	15.8	156-334	.467	0-2	107-152	.704	419	5.5	16
Hodges	73	11.5	146-344	.424	44-115	26-27	.963	362	5.0	20
Hopson	61	11.9	104-244	.426	1-5	55-83	.663	264	4.3	14
Perdue	74	13.1	116-235	.494	0-3	75-112	.670	307	4.1	15
Levingston	78	13.0	127-282	.450	1-4	59-91	.648	314	4.0	14
Williams	51	6.6	53-104	.510	1-2	20-28	.714	127	2.5	10
Team	82	240.9	3632-7125	.510	155-424	1605-2111	.760	9024	110.0	155
Opponents	82	240.9	3267-6884	.475	190-626	1554-2017	.770	8278	101.0	145

Player	Off Reb	Def Reb	Tot Reb	Reb Avg	Ast	Ast Avg	PF	FO	Stl	To	Blk
Jordan	118	374	492	6.0	453	5.5	229	1	223	202	83
Pippen	163	432	595	7.3	511	6.2	270	3	193	232	93
Grant	266	393	659	8.4	178	2.3	203	2	95	92	69
Cartwright	167	319	486	6.2	126	1.6	167	0	32	113	15
Armstrong	25	124	149	1.8	301	3.7	118	0	70	107	4
Paxson	15	76	91	1.1	297	3.6	136	0	62	69	3
King	72	136	208	2.7	65	0.9	134	0	24	91	42
Hodges	10	32	42	0.6	97	1.3	74	0	34	35	2
Hopson	49	60	109	1.8	65	1.1	79	0	25	59	14
Perdue	122	214	336	4.5	47	0.6	147	1	23	75	57
Levingston	99	126	225	2.9	56	0.7	143	0	29	50	43
Williams	42	56	98	1.9	16	0.3	51	0	12	23	13
Team	1148	2342	3490	42.6	2212	27.0	1751	7	822	1184	438
Opponents	1062	2162	3224	39.3	2016	24.6	1826	17	633	1402	348

NBA Finals
Year By Year

YEAR WINNER (COACH)	LOSER (COACH)	GAMES
1947 Philadelphia Warriors (Gottlieb)	Chicago Stags (Olsen)	4-1
1948 Baltimore Bullets (Jeannette)	Philadelphia Warriors (Gottlieb)	4-2
1949 Minneapolis Lakers (Kundla)	Washington Capitols (Auerbach)	4-2
1950 Minneapolis Lakers (Kundla)	*Syracuse Nationals (Cervi)	4-2
1951 Rochester Royals (Harrison)	N.Y. Knicks (Lapchick)	4-3
1952 Minneapolis Lakers (Kundla)	N.Y. Knicks (Lapchick)	4-3
1953 *Minneapolis Lakers (Kundla)	N.Y. Knicks (Lapchick)	4-1
1954 *Minneapolis Lakers (Kundla)	Syracuse (Cervi)	4-3
1955 *Syracuse Nationals (Cervi)	*Ft. Wayne Pistons (Eckman)	4-3
1956 *Philadelphia (Senesky)	Ft. Wayne Pistons (Eckman)	4-1
1957 *Boston Celtics (Auerbach)	St. Louis Hawks (Hannum)	4-3
1958 St. Louis Hawks (Hannum)	*Boston Celtics (Auerbach)	4-2
1959 *Boston Celtics (Auerbach)	Minneapolis Lakers (Kundla)	4-0
1960 *Boston Celtics (Auerbach)	St. Louis Hawks (Macauley)	4-3
1961 *Boston Celtics (Auerbach)	St. Louis Hawks (Seymour)	4-1
1962 *Boston Celtics (Auerbach)	L.A. Lakers (Schaus)	4-3
1963 *Boston Celtics (Auerbach)	L.A. Lakers (Schaus)	4-2
1964 *Boston Celtics (Auerbach)	San Francisco Warriors (Hannum)	4-1
1965 *Boston Celtics (Auerbach)	L.A. Lakers (Schaus)	4-1
1966 Boston Celtics (Auerbach)	L.A. Lakers (Schaus)	4-2
1967 *Philadelphia 76ers (Hannum)	San Francisco Warriors (Sharman)	4-2
1968 Boston Celtics (Russell)	L.A. Lakers (van Breda Kolff)	4-2
1969 Boston Celtics (Russell)	L.A. Lakers (van Breda Kolff)	4-3
1970 *N.Y. Knicks (Holzman)	L.A. Lakers (Mullaney)	4-3
1971 *Milwaukee Bucks (Costello)	Baltimore Bullets (Shue)	4-0
1972 *L.A. Lakers (Sharman)	N.Y. Knicks (Holzman)	4-1
1973 N.Y. Knicks (Holzman)	L.A. Lakers (Sharman)	4-1
1974 Boston Celtics (Heinsohn)	*Milwaukee Bucks (Costello)	4-3
1975 Golden State Warriors (Attles)	*Washington Bullets (Jones)	4-0
1976 Boston Celtics (Heinsohn)	Phoenix Suns (MacLeod)	4-2
1977 Portland Trail Blazers (Ramsay)	Philadelphia 76ers (Shue)	4-2
1978 Washington Bullets (Motta)	Seattle SuperSonics (Wilkens)	4-3
1979 Seattle SuperSonics (Wilkens)	*Washington Bullets (Motta)	4-1
1980 L.A. Lakers (Westhead)	Philadelphia 76ers (Cunningham)	4-2
1981 *Boston Celtics (Fitch)	Houston Rockets (Harris)	4-2
1982 L.A. Lakers (Riley)	Philadelphia 76ers (Cunningham)	4-2
1983 *Phil. 76ers (Cunningham)	L.A. Lakers (Riley)	4-0
1984 *Boston Celtics (Jones)	L.A. Lakers (Riley)	4-3
1985 L.A. Lakers (Riley)	*Boston Celtics (Jones)	4-2
1986 *Boston Celtics (Jones)	Houston Rockets (Fitch)	4-2
1987 *L.A. Lakers (Riley)	Boston Celtics (Jones)	4-2
1988 *L.A. Lakers (Riley)	Detroit Pistons (Daly)	4-3
1989 *Detroit Pistons (Daly)	L.A. Lakers (Riley)	4-0
1990 Detroit Pistons (Daly)	Portland Trail Blazers (Adelman)	4-1
1991 **BULLS** (Jackson)	L.A. Lakers (Dunleavy)	4-1

*Had best record (or tied for best record) during regular season.

Bulls milestones

Nobody could have written a better script for the Bulls. They waited until this, their 25th year, to set the following club records:

■ Won city's first NBA championship.

■ Advanced into the championship finals.

■ Won 61 regular-season games.

■ Drew 757,745 fans, which averages out to a standing-room Stadium crowd of 18,482 for each home game.

■ Finished with the Eastern Conference's best regular season record of 61-21.

■ Accomplished their first 3-0 and 4-0 playoff sweeps in team history.

■ Had a player (Michael Jordan) win a fifth consecutive league scoring title.

■ Qualified for their seventh playoff.

■ Won their 1,000th game, a 99-89 home victory over the Utah Jazz Feb. 8.

■ Drew their 10 millionth fan.

■ Won 26 consecutive home games.

■ Scored their most points (155) in regulation beating the Phoenix Suns 155-127 Dec. 4, 1990. Those points also featured club records for field goals (67) in a game, field goals in a half (35), points in a half (86), points in a quarter (46), points (282) and field goals made (119) by two teams.

■ Had their best month with an 11-1 February.

■ Played their 1,000th home game, April 7 against Philadelphia.

■ Held the Cleveland Cavaliers to a record five points in the first quarter, Dec. 15.

■ Scored a record 26 consecutive points in the 116-98 victory over the Cavs on Dec. 15.

■ Extended their home sellout streak to 181 regular-season games.

■ Leased a full-time private charter plane, MGM Grand, for all road games for the whole season.

■ Led the league beating opponents by a club-record average margin of 9.1 points a game.

Lacy J. Banks

Autographs